Born for Each Other

by

BLANCA MOORE

iUniverse, Inc.
New York   Bloomington

iUniverse books may be ordered through booksellers or by contacting:

iUniverse
1663 Liberty Drive
Bloomington, IN 47403
www.iuniverse.com
1-800-Authors (1-800-288-4677)

Because of the dynamic nature of the Internet, any Web addresses or links contained in this book may have changed since publication and may no longer be valid. The views expressed in this work are solely those of the author and do not necessarily reflect the views of the publisher, and the publisher hereby disclaims any responsibility for them.

ISBN: 978-1-4401-2792-2 (sc)
ISBN: 978-1-4401-2793-9 (ebook)

Printed in the United States of America

iUniverse rev. date: 03/20/2009

Dedication

To my husband:
I feel my life started the moment I saw him.
For the love we shared.

To my children:
Jimmy and Lois, because they are
The continuation of Jimmy and my love to each other

To my Grandchildren:
Because they have been the joy of our life

To Earl:
You have been loved in our home, as much of
our children have been

To Kelvin:
Thank you for the love you have given our daughter and
To our family

Prelude

One afternoon, I was walking along with a friend of mine from work. As we stopped To wait for the traffic so that we could cross the street, I noticed a Chevrolet pick-up, no reason I should have noticed the truck. There were everywhere, and there was not any reason why I should have notice this particular one. As we waited for the driver to turn so that we could cross and get out of the hot sun, he looked my way hoping for a clear shot to make his turn, and was struck by his eyes, beautiful blue/grey big eyes.

I asked my friend, "Did you see that man's eyes?"

She said. "No."

He was wearing a short sleeves dark peach/brown sport shirt with buttons on the sleeves. And never thought I would ever see him again.

Chapter One

My name is Blanca Jimenez; I was born in Coatzacoalcos, Veracruz, Mexico. I had very good parents, and only one sister, Reyna Violeta.

My parents were very strict, but good nature people, my Daddy used to play jokes on everyone in the family and then laughed about it. He used to set the table and give my Aunt Lucha cooking utensils to eat with. Everybody would wait for her to come to the table and look at her face when she saw her table setting. Also, when we ate, and someone asked to pass the salt, he literally passed the salt in front of your face and would ask, "I passed the salt, do you want me to pass it again?"

But when it was time to be strict, our curfew time was ten p. m. People didn't start arriving at a dance until nine p.m. but we couldn't make him understand it wasn't enough time to stay at a party, but if my Aunt Lucha went with us as a chaperone, we could stay until 1 a.m.

Coatzacoalcos was the biggest city in the South of the State of Veracruz and the largest city in the South where Pemex, (Mexico's oil company) had their main offices; there were three main offices in the country, at that time, Mexico City, Monterrey for the North and Coatzacoalcos for the South part of the country. There was a lot of work in the Coatzacoalcos area, lots of Industries there.

I started to learn English in junior high, and from then on I was hooked, I took private lessons where ever there were offered. I kept studying English, perhaps because my father went to school in the United States and spoke very good English.

My father went to the Allis Chalmers Technical School in Oregon and for many years they were the leading heavy equipment machinery in the world. My father was the only person in the South of Mexico who was an expert in that kind of heavy machinery, at that time; when he went back to Mexico after he finished school, he worked for Pemex in the Coatzacoalcos area.

My sister is older than I, but only by eighteen months, it was enough that when she went out with her friends, she didn't want me to go with her I would be out of place, age wise. (she was fifteen years old and had her (quinceañera party, I was only thirteen), but she wasn't allowed to go without me. This infuriated her.

She always studied piano, I, on the other hand, wanted to play it, but hated to study, so while she played beautifully, she played in concerts and was the background music for ballet recitals. When we got older, we also got closer to each other; we have remained close to this day.

My sister met Miguel Rustrian, a civil engineer at a dance and soon became engaged. Miguel said he didn't believe in long engagements and wanted to get married within three months. Miguel didn't have an ounce of good sense of humor in his body, in contrast with my sister, a very happy person with a smile in her face at all times. If it's true that opposites attract each other, it came true in their case. Within three months of becoming engaged they were married.

My sister was a very pretty bride in the dress made especially for her; it lace and tulle, long sleeves blouse made out of lace, lace skirt with tulle inserted in it. Conchita Nettel and I were her maiden of honor. We have a ceremony where a lasso goes around the bride and groom and are united with it, it's called the "velacion" they put a candle on each side of bride and groom.

Blanca, her sister Reyna Violeta, with their parents, Reina and Francisco Jimenez

I start my story in May 1962, after my father had passed away the year before, with my sister married and moved away from home. I worked for an American company as a bilingual secretary, I was well known in the working circuit because they were not too many bilingual secretaries in the area.

A friend of the family came over to invite us to a Baptism of a mutual friend's baby, I hesitated to accept, but I finally accepted the invitation because he was the godfather and my Aunt Lucha was my "chaperone" for the day; we could not have gone to a party without one. That was the first time I had gone to a party since my father died.

I wore a silk cream color dress, neck line was low cut; the full skirt had a fabric embroider flowers of the same color and a pearl necklace.

There were a lot of people when we arrived. Lots of girls everywhere, as usual, not too many men. So, when they played something to dance with, ten to fifteen girls circled around this American man, just teasing him, he didn't know what to do, so I hollered to him, from the outside of the circle, "Do you need any help?" I said to him, in English.

He answered, "Yes," he was very relieved to get out of the circle of girls. He took my hand and smiled, and he never let my hand go, not ever again. His name was James Moore, but everyone called him Shorty. He wasn't very tall. He had a smile that stayed with me forever. Then I recognized him to be the man I admired in the street a few weeks earlier. And I saw his eyes closer and I was right there looking at the most beautiful eyes I had ever seen in my life. I melted every time he looked at me.

We just sat and talk the whole time. I was glad he didn't invite me to dance because I felt uncomfortable just being there since this was the first time I have been out to a party since my father died the year before.

He told me "I work for Permargo, an oil company, do you know the company I'm talking about?" "Yes, I do." I told him. "I work for Zapata, as a bilingual secretary". I said. "I used to work for Zapata." He said smiling, "I came to Coatzacoalcos with Zapata, but when they were here before, their contract ended and they went back to the States. A friend of mine owns Permargo and he asked me to stay with his company. Since I wanted to stay in Mexico. I did."

There was a restaurant and night club around the corner. The Lemarroy Hotel, on the top of the Hotel they built a night club, the Caravelle, Jimmy said, "There is a band playing there tonight, do you and your Aunt would like to come with me?" I asked my aunt, and she said it would be all right. So we went, we walked in. there was a bright moon that night, I don't remember if I have been there before, we sat by the dance floor, I remember every time I looked at the people who were dancing, Jimmy would turn my face towards him so he would get my undivided attention. There was this dancer who came out half naked, I could have died, I was so embarrassed. Jimmy felt bad he had talked us into going there, but my aunt was amused because she knew how I felt in front of this man I hardly knew and this half naked dancer, I turned my face the other way the whole time the dancer was on the floor. When she left. Jimmy apologized to me for taking us there. I told him "I know you didn't know who the entertainer would be."

The next day, while was at work, I saw him coming into my office, I was surprised to see him; he hadn't said anything the night before about coming in to my office.

"Hi," he said smiling, "do you like to go to lunch with me?" "I have to call home," I told him, "my mother is expecting me for lunch." I had to send a messenger, because at that time, not too many homes had a private phone. In the meantime, Jimmy visited with my boss, Mr. Mel Morgan; they knew each other since Jimmy had worked for that company in the past. Then he turned to me and said, "What did your mother said?"

"She said it's all right by her." I told him.

On the way out he asked me, "Do you like Gloria's restaurant?" "Yes, I do. But I haven't been there in a long time. It'll be nice." Some of his friends from work were there and began to tease him because they have not ever seen him with a girl before. He introduced me to them, but then ushered me to another table.

He had to leave later that day; he worked in an off-shore drilling rig as a tool pusher. I didn't think much about the whole thing, that is, until the following week when he came back. He took me to lunch, after I got out from work he picked me up, took me home, we visited there, he spoke little Spanish, he met my mama, Reina, every one called Reyita, but me of course. He also met my Grandmother, my other Aunt Quina, and her daughter Rosa del Carmen, we all called her Rosi.

On Saturday he invited me to go to Lake Catemaco, a beautiful place not far from Coatzacoalcos, of course my mama went with us; there was no question about us going alone. We could see Catemaco from the top of the mountain; you can see the lake below and the town around it. Then as you drive into the town, the road winds and it's a beautiful scene. A great many people travel there just for the scenery. We have several pictures, all taken by my mother. It was a beautiful sunny day, we walked by the edge of the high hill side and my mother took many pictures of us. Jimmy started calling my mother "mama", and my mother would tell him, "not yet, Jimmy." Lots of people go to Catemaco, because of the beautiful scenery and because there is a Church there of Our Lady of Carmen, many miracles have been attributed to her.

Jimmy would come and visit me at home with my family; he knew I couldn't just go every night and he accepted our ways. We lived in a duplex; one side was ours, the other side, my Grandmother, Aunts, and cousins. My Aunt Lucha was from my Grandmother's first marriage, she became a widow at 21 years old, my Aunt Lucha never married. My Grandmother remarried a man from the Canary Islands, the largest island of the Canary Islands; Albino Cruz. My mother was their first child, then my Aunt Quina, my Uncle Albino was their youngest one. My Grandfather was a river Pilot in Coatza-coalcos. My cousins Rosa Maria and Clara Luz were the daughters of my Uncle Albino and Rosi was the daughter of my Aunt Quina. I remember as a child, we had company once, and my uncle and this other man were talking, and he asked my Uncle, "Are you the youngest one?" to which my uncle replied, "I used to be, but now I'm told I'm the oldest one."

My Grandmother had almost completely lost her eyesight to a couple of cataracts. She had always been an avid reader, I remember growing up, since she no longer was able to read, all of her Granddaughters would fight each other for the privilege of reading to our Grandmother.

Any more, as soon as Jimmy came into town, he went straight to my office and we would go to lunch to the Gloria's restaurant. One day, he said, "let's go to this store, it seems they have everything." We went; it was "La Nueva China", we looked, and we found a model battleship, "we can put this together, I think it will be fun." He said. It will give us something to do while we visit at home. My mother would bring us a cup of coffee and my Aunt Lucha would bring us a piece of cake. She baked often and loved to bake. Jimmy tried to talk to my mother, grandmother and my aunts. Rosi was another story, she was our regular chaperone, and Jimmy liked Rosi a whole lot, they teased each other all the time. But with his limited Spanish and her lack of English there were not too many conversations.

Rosi would ask Jimmy: "Hey!, when are you going to take me to the movies?" and he would respond, "Just pick the movie up and we'll go."

Sometimes when we leave the house, Jimmy would tell my mother, "Mama, see you in two or three days." And my mama would tell Jimmy, "Don't be naughty, Jimmy." Jimmy would be satisfied he had a conversation with my mother. Sometimes my Grandmother would come to the door when it was a little later than usual, and said in a loud voice, "is that man still there?" It would embarrass me, but Jimmy thought it was funny. Jimmy seemed to prefer our home atmosphere to visit, than to go to restaurants and sit at their tables to visit.

Our routine to have lunch at Gloria's restaurant became so regular, than when we didn't go for a few days and then went back, they would all asked where have we been, but the truth was, my mother cooked lunch for us, sometimes.

Jimmy came back from one of his trips from the rig all excited because he had seen some people dig out a stone head in La Venta, Tabasco. It was over six feet tall Olmeca stone head. It was a one piece stone with big eyes, a big nose and thick lips. One of the latest findings in the country, at that time. Olmecas was an Indian tribe in Veracruz and Tabasco. He watched them dig it out from the original site. That was really something; he was very excited about it because he was very interested in ancient history. The fact he watched them dig it out off the ground, was rare. He was very proud about it. Several months later, we saw the stone outside the courthouse in Coatzacoalcos. Years later, we saw it at the Museum of history in Houston.

One evening, Jimmy and I went to the park. One of the rare occasions we were alone. It was early in the evening and the park was deserted; we sat by the entrance, that's when he told me about his life. He had been married and had one son, Earl, who was seven years old; Jimmy was waiting for the divorce to be final. I told him. "I can't go out with you anymore, you are a married man." He said, "No, I'm not, I am just waiting for the papers to come through, the reason I can't precipitate things is because the woman was married to, had a boyfriend, and she is expecting his baby, now," he said, "do you understand that I had no part in the arrangement?"

He held my hand, "Blanca, I love you and I'm telling you the truth, (thinking back, I loved him too, but I didn't know how it felt) I left my hand in his, I trembled, my God, I thought, what is this? I stood up and started to walk, he followed me, "Blanca," he said, "Did you hear what I said? I love you."

"Yes, I heard you, but right now, I'm very confuse James, I know I like you very much, I'm just confuse about the situation, you understand, don't you?" he just nodded. He said. I have not talked to anyone about this, but I want you to know about me, and I want to get to know you, I feel I know you forever even if we have known each other but a little while." He took both of my hands and looked straight into my eyes and said "I love you, Blanca," I looked at him and looked down, I didn't know what to say, I didn't how I felt, my heart raced every time he looked at me, my hands trembled every time he touched me, if that was love, then I was madly in love with him. "Can we see each other again?" he asked me. "Yes, we can see each other again." But I have to think about this James, you know I'm catholic and I can't go out with married men." "Blanca, I'm no longer a married man, otherwise I wouldn't have approached you if it wasn't so, believe me." We left the park and he took me home. For some reason I didn't tell my mother or anyone else about my conversation with Jimmy that night. The park was empty, it wasn't late, but it was the middle of the week, the perfect time for the kind of conversation we had just had.

I continued to see him; something drew me to him more and more until he was the only one I thought about. For the very first time in my life, I knew in my heart I was in love, really and truly in love. When I told my mother about my conversation with Jimmy that night, my mama fought me from the first time she suspected I loved him, worse yet, he was divorced! And from another country! She was dead set against me seeing Jimmy again.

She used to tell me, "Blanca, if he marries you, he will take you away from here, I don't want you to go away." To which I would replied, "Well, Reyna Violeta lives in Mexico City, you don't see her very often." She said, "yes, but she is in our country. I don't want you to go to another country. I'll never see you again. I don't want you to go that far. We don't know who he is or who his family is." I said to her. "Yes, like the Solers, everybody knew who he was, and what happened? He killed himself on their wedding night and left his bride. He left her in a lot of trouble; everybody knew his family, didn't they? So she couldn't top that. She just nodded her head.

I still remember the Solers, one of the oldest families in Coatzacoalcos, my own sister was named after the groom's mother because they were such good friends. Everybody was happy with that match; both families were well known in the community, after a lavish wedding celebration, they left on their honeymoon in their car with a private driver to their hotel to an unspecified location. The next day, the newspaper was full of news, the outline of their wedding, and the news about the groom's death. It was very tragic for everyone. When I heard about the death of the groom, I went to their home, the wires of congratulations and condolences were mixed. The bride was loved and what happened to her was felt by everyone in the State. I only mention this because my mother didn't want me to marry Jimmy, only because no one knew his family and I had to show to her that, that is no reason to stop someone from marrying the person they love.

We lived like that, Jimmy worked one week and one week on shore. Once when he was off, he came to the States on business, the Judge who handled his divorce had cited him to come to the United States for an appointment to finalize the arrangements for child support and visitation rights. Earl's mother charged Jimmy with not paying child support, but Jimmy went prepared for it and displayed check stubs for paid checks cashed by her, for more than she said he had not paid. The Judge gave him credit for that amount and told him he didn't have to pay for several months afterwards, but he continued paying every month after that.

He brought me back a record, it was titled "The Great Pretender", by The Platters; they were very popular then (1962). My boss, for reasons I didn't understand, despised Jimmy, when he saw the title of the record he brought was "The Great Pretender, he started to yell all over the office, "Yes, that's what he is, a great pretender." Jimmy just laughed when I told him, and shook his head.

We played "The Platters" every time he came back from work, we loved "Smoke gets in your eyes", we danced to it every chance we had, he sang it to me; he didn't think he could sing, but I always thought he had a good voice. He also sang "One in a Million" to me and then he'll said, "that's what you are baby, one in a million and I found you."

I realized that while he was away, I was lost without him; soon after he came back from the States, I found out he drank. I didn't know how much, I suspect if I had known I really wouldn't have cared. I knew then all I ever wanted was to be with him, just holding hands was enough to make my heart pound faster. We were chaperone during most of our dates, and were never more intimate than sharing a simple kiss. But occasionally we could escape our chaperone and go for a drive, alone. It was then when we could kiss like we wanted to freely and passionately. And then, one night we went to the Malecon. Jimmy asked me. "Blanca, you know how much I love you, will you marry me?" I said. "Yes, James, I will marry you." We kissed and kissed, and then he pulled back and told me, you don't know how much I love you, Blanca." "I love you, James, very much." We stayed like that in one long embraced.

"A few days later, he told me he was leaving Mexico soon, I knew it was matter of time, all the other Americans had left, Jimmy was one of the few that were still there. One thing that worried him was that I was twenty four years old, he was thirty six, but that was never important to me.

Jimmy didn't know enough Spanish to ask my mother for my hand in marriage, so I had to tell her myself, she cried and cried, begged me not to marry Jimmy. "I said, mama, you know I have never loved anyone, I will never love anyone else, I was born for him." She bowed her head and nodded.

My Aunts and my Grandmother were happy for me, I guess mama was happy too, in a way, but she cried a lot. The company I worked for, finished their contract and left Coatzacoalcos, so I took another job, also for a big company, Guanos y Fertilizantes de Mexico, I worked there until I married Jimmy. Jimmy was there in Coatzacoalcos for about one year after we started going together before the Americans from all the oil Companies started to leave Mexico. When Jimmy started to get ready to leave, he brought me a box of books that he had inherited from the other Americans that had already left. He told me there were good to practice my English.

Before he left, Jimmy brought a couple of his friends, Linda and Hank Murray, very nice people from Baton Rouge, La. He worked for a new company out of Villahermosa, Tabasco. But after they met us kept coming on a daily basis, by then, most American people had left and so we began a good friendship that lasted many years.

It was time for Jimmy to leave and he promised me to write often and he left, leaving me with the promise that he would come back as soon as he could get a job in the States and got situated. He talked to my mother the best way he could, he told her: "Mama, "(he called her Mama from the start) "I'm coming back for Blanquita," he told her, I wish I could take with me now, but she knows there is no job waiting for me in the States, and I have to wait for that. I will come back for her as soon as I can." I didn't want to go to the airport. I knew how much I would cry and I didn't want to see me like that.

I never doubted him. But everybody laughed at me behind my back because I didn't want to date anyone, and when we went to a dance, I would tell whoever invited me to dance, that I had a boyfriend. No one ever thought he would come back for me. My friends would tell me, "Why do you tell everybody you have a boyfriend that may never come back for you?" "But he will come back." I would tell them. They would replied, "Do you know how many girls believed that? They boyfriends never came back, Blanca." It was very hard when your friends talk to you like that.

It was 1963 and the job situation was bad in the States, Jimmy found small jobs on land rigs, but nothing that allow him to save enough money to live on, pay child support and still save enough money to come back to Mexico for me.

Then Linda Murray, the American lady, and a good friend of my family, was coming to the States, I begged Mama to let me come with her. She lived in Baton Rouge, La. So either Jimmy had to go to Louisiana to see me or I had to go to Texas, to visit with him, and I could meet his family.

Mama let me go, after all, I was twenty four years old by then, but she knew I wouldn't have gone without her permission. Jimmy went to Baton Rouge to see me. Oh, I was in heaven.

When he arrived, I open the passenger door and got in, we kissed. He was only able to be there a couple of days because of his job. Linda's family used to go to their lake cabin on the weekend trips to fish, the cabin was at False River, not far from Baton Rouge, I remember on the way to the cabin the huge trees cover with what I was told were magnolia flowers, huge white beautiful flowers. Louisiana State flower. But we were going fishing, and Jimmy loved to fish, the family lend Jimmy a fishing rod and we were on our way to fish. We had a great time while he was there. Miss Sally, Linda's mother was a delight to visit with, and we visited a lot with her. Then it was time for Jimmy to leave, and I was just devastated. But consoled myself that at least, we had seen each other.

Mrs. Murray had a son living in Dallas, so like it or not, I went to Dallas even if where I wanted to go was Kountze to visit with Jimmy. But my friend said no, and reminded me that Mama would not had approved. I finally convinced her by telling her my trip was to see Jimmy, I didn't care seeing anything or anyone else.

I talk to Jimmy over the phone several times, then we agreed when was the best time for me to go to see him in Texas. The following week I went to Beaumont, Texas. Jimmy met me at the bus station, he smiled and held my hand, he said, "Hello, doll", and kissed me. He took me for a long ride all the way to Dam B on the way to Kountze. Now I know how long that ride was. I remember wild flowers of all colors covering the fields, lots of trees, very different vegetation that what I had just seen in Louisiana. He parked by the dam. He told me he wanted to talk to me before we went to his parents' house, and his mother needed the time to cook lunch. The trip from Beaumont to Kountze its only thirty miles, the trip from Beaumont to Dam B (a well known lake close to Jasper, Texas) it's about 75 miles, he told me he wanted to show me part of Texas.

He also wanted to explain to me why he couldn't let me stay and get married, which it was what we both wanted. He still didn't have a steady job; he needed a good job to do the things he needed to do. Then he took me to his parents' home to eat lunch. I remember I wore a blue and white striped dress, one of my favorite dresses. When we arrived to his parents' home, he said: "This is Blanquita." His mother took a step and embraced me.

His parents owned a filling station-grocery store, it was in front of the property which it was a large corner adjacent to three highways, the house was kind of at the back of the property, a beautiful white frame large house. I was to spend the night at his parents' house, Jimmy's mama was a beautiful person, and very sweet to me. Everyone was very nice to me, and I was very happy.

Jimmy's mother cooked a very elaborate lunch, cornbread dressing with pork chops on top, asparagus, mashed potatoes, green beans and biscuits, and a couple of pies, and everything was delicious. Mr. Moore asked what kind of ice cream did I like. I liked them all, I said. He left and came back a few minutes later with several half gallon cartons of ice cream.

Jimmy's oldest brother Merle, and a younger brother, Don, ran the station. There were seven brothers, Merle was the oldest, then Jack, living in Louisiana with his wife Elmarie, then was Jimmy, next was Bert (Corky) who lived in Nederland with his wife Adele, Don, Robert and Darrell, whom everybody called Tyke, they were not married at the time.

Merle and Don were the only brothers in Kountze, and they couldn't do enough for me. Jimmy took me for a ride around town that night. There were grave markers on one corner to advertise; Jimmy said to me, "my brother Tyke said this town it's so dead, they used grave markers for street signs."

I had a great time, and then it was time to leave. Jimmy told me "I have an appointment with an oil company in Houston. The one I worked for before, (it was Zapata off-shore, the same company I worked for in Coatzacoalcos), and he thought he could go overseas with them; he'll let me know how it went. So he took me to the bus station in Beaumont and I left for Baton Rouge. The same week, Mrs. Murray and I went back to Mexico.

After I went back to Mexico, the waiting was harder and then his letter came, he had gotten an overseas job, in Borneo! I wanted to die.

So, he was off to Borneo, we corresponded often, he wrote to me every week, his mama started writing to me. That's how I started corresponding with my future mother-in-law, and I learned to call her mama, because that's how she signed her letters to me, mama. She wrote me "Write me, because that's the only way I'll know about Teeny (Jimmy's family nickname) he wouldn't write to me nearly as often as to you, she said, I remember on the first letter she wrote: We enjoyed your company very much, and I know you'll like it here when you and Teeny get married. Love, mama. Let me tell you, I enjoyed that letter tremendously. For a longtime, I kept it in my purse and read it every chance I had.

I wrote Jimmy twice a week. I started reading some of the books he left me; I had a dictionary to help me out when I ran into trouble with a word. When I started reading Madam Chatter-something, I ran into a problem, There was a word I couldn't find in any dictionary, it started with an "f", so when I wrote Jimmy I asked him, "what does it mean? I can't find out." I said to him.

In the meantime, Mrs. Murray came over to visit, Good, I thought, "I need to know what this word means," I said to her. "I wrote to Jimmy asking him, but there no telling when I get an answer." She yelled when I showed her the book, laughed and laughed out loud when she saw the word, she said, "and you asked Shorty?" I said, yes, "I couldn't find out any other way." "Well, write him again and tell him I am here now, and you don't need an explanation from him." So I did.

He wrote me once asking me if I could go to Borneo so we could get married over there. My mama said, "no way." I really didn't want to go around the world to get married. That's was not the way I pictured myself getting married. Overseas contracts were for two years, for drilling personnel, so we were for a long wait.

We were trying to figure out how we could get married sooner, when I received a letter from Jimmy, he wrote: "Baby, our problems are over, the company I work for sold the rig and we are all going back to the United States. I am coming over so we can get married. "That would make it in December. I couldn't believe it, and neither could anybody else, for different reasons, I was surprised and thankful my prayers had been answered.

I went to Mexico City to buy my wedding attire, I ordered invitations for the wedding, then I waited to hear from Jimmy because he didn't know when he could leave Borneo, also, flights from Singapore were not daily.

When the invitations arrived, everybody gathered around the dining room table to address the invitations from a long list we had prepared, we had to leave blank, date and time to fill out later.

I also had to go to the Courthouse, one of my teachers from High School was the Mayor at the time and he gave a special permit to get married in Church without the civil ceremony, that's the equivalent of the Justice of the Peace. He asked me. "Do you think he'll marry you in the Courthouse once you get there?" "I know he will." I told him.

My cousins and my friends organized a bridal shower for me; it was great, all my friends were there, the house was full. Our bridal showers are all jokes for the bride and just mock gifts and a lot of fun.

My mother and I went to San Andres Tuxtla to ask the Bishop for a special dispensation to get married to someone who is not Catholic; he did immediately because he knew me very well through my work with the church. I remember when we went back to Coatzacoalcos, there was a Pilgrimage procession for Our Lady Guadalupe, since the festivities had started that night, everyone was holding a candle, we were given our candle and we started walking with the procession to the Church.

It was very hard to get a phone call through from Singapore, at that time, so he would call me when he arrived in the United States. The call came. He would fly to Minatitlan, that's where the airport was for Coatzacoalcos. He was to arrive on Sunday the 13th of December 1964, we still had to fill in the date and time in the invitations, the envelopes were ready, we had a lot of help, and we mailed everything the same day. We had to get married the next day because Jimmy had to go to work to following week. It was Monday December 14, 1964.

We picked Jimmy up at the airport, all my family and Mr. Murray, who was Jimmy's Best Man, Mrs. Murray had already left to go home for Christmas, were there. And then, I saw Jimmy coming out of the plane, my heart stopped. He came to me and said, "Hi doll." And kissed me long and hard, and I didn't care who saw us.

I was in the car with Jimmy and Mr. Murray, we stopped at Jimmy's hotel so he could get a room and drop his suitcase, my cousins went ahead and went home, my cousin Rosi went in running and shouting "Shorty wasn't in the plane." My mother sat down before she fainted, "No," she said, "Shorty needed to get a room at the hotel, they're behind us. My poor mama was about to pass out."

Rosi was well known for her sense was humor; she always played jokes on people and laughed about it. Besides that, she was Jimmy's best friend because she chaperoned us most of the time.

We went to Church that afternoon, I had taken the special dispensation I had gotten from the Bishop, but the new Priest didn't want to accept anything, he said, "the fact that your boyfriend had been married before don't set right with me." I said to him. "I was taught all my life you are married only if you marry in the Church; before the eyes of God, a marriage before a Justice of the Peace doesn't count in Church, why are you counting that now? Well," I said, "he came to marry me just as he promised he was going to do, all the way from Borneo, and if you don't marry us, I'm leaving with him."

The Priest looked at me and walked away, he walked back and forth, and then, he came back and said "I'll see you in the morning." In the meantime, there was another Priest I knew from a long time ago, Padre Elfrego, he told me, "Don't worry Blanca, if he doesn't want to marry you, my Church its less than one hour from here, I'll marry you."

That night, Mr. Murray, my bother-in-law Miguel, Octavio, who is Rosa Maria's husband and Juan Medina, a family friend, took Jimmy to the Lemarroy hotel for drinks, that was supposed to have been Jimmy's bachelor party.

There was a lady friend of ours, Mrs. Vasquez; Jimmy was a good friend of her husband. When she came for the wedding, she told me; "when Jimmy and I met, at that party, Jimmy was talking to her, he was telling her about his bad experience and that he would never marry again, right at that moment, she said, you walked in." Jimmy said, "oh, oh, I think I am going have to change my mind." "And by God, he did." She hugged me, and said. "I'm so happy for you both."

The ceremony was at 8:30 a.m. the next day, it had rained all night, but it was a beautiful morning, Jimmy and Mr. Murray were supposed to meet us at the church, right? Wrong, they were at my house before 8:00 a.m. "Oh, my God," everyone said, they ran around the house, "Jimmy is here, he is here, tell him to go to church. Don't let him see Blanca." Everybody was trying to tell him to go to church, Jimmy flatly refused. "No, I'm going to church with Blanquita."

He rode in the car with me, everyone laughed when they saw the groom getting out of the bride's car, instead of the bride, then he gave me his hand, and I got out. The church was full, I guess no one believed he would come, others didn't remember to whom I was marrying.

My dress was made out of a heavy satin in a pearl shade, high neck and long sleeves, covered buttons down the back of the blouse, straight skirt, sequenced lace, up to the knees, split back skirt. The chapel train detachable below the waist. My veil was down to my hips and my hair piece was made out of azahar flowers going around my head. Low heel lined shoes, to match the dress.

The church was beautifully decorated with white gladiolas along the aisle and up to the Altar, at the top of the Altar was the Lady of Guadalupe, below was our Lady of Carmen. The bridal procession consisted of my maiden of honor, were my sister Reyna Violeta, and all my cousins, Rosa Maria, Clara Luz, and Rosa del Carmen.

Then my Godmother for baptism, Rosa Eva del Alto, and my God-mother for First Communion, Aida Vargas, were my Godmother of lasso, a Spanish costume where bride and groom are united by the lasso, split in the middle, mine was a giant rosary, one side goes to the bride's shoulder, the other on the groom's shoulder. I always thought it is a beautiful costume. Its call, the Vigil Ceremony. (The Velacion.)

It was a beautiful ceremony, although I had to bump Jimmy on the side to let him know when to say "I do". He was scared to be there among so many people, he knew he was the center of atten-tion, other than the bride, in a way; he was more of a curiosity than the bride.

James and Blanca, on their wedding day.

Everybody in the family was in the wedding party, Jimmy was very nervous and if it hadn't been because he knew what it meant for me to be married in the Church he wouldn't have consented to do it. In fact, there was never questioned whether it was going to be done. Jimmy waited at the Altar with Mr. Murray, and Miguel, my brother-in-law walked me to the Altar.

My cake was beautiful, it was a clover shaped, on one leaf, was the Bible, on another, a rosary, another one was the bouquet, another had the rings; I thought it was the most beautiful cake I had ever seen, and very original. One of my cousins, Maria de los Angeles Lara, made the cake. She did a beautiful job. We had a small reception at my house. After all, it was early in the morning. Before I took my wedding gown off, it was time for my Grandmother's blessing; we knelt in front of her on a pillow they had prepared. I can still see my wonderful Grandmother's face. Everyone gathered around to pray for our happiness.

Our flight was at 1:30 p.m. By that time it was raining a lot, they announced the plane was circling over the airport, but because of the storm couldn't land, they were not sure it would land at all that day. My mother came running to where I was and announced to me that, "If the plane doesn't land, you're not going anywhere with that man." I told Jimmy what mama had said, "You just tell mama your name is not Jimenez anymore; you are a Moore now."

The plane finally landed and we left for Mexico City, we had to sit where there was an empty seat, so we had to sit apart from each other, I was sitting next to a Nun who noticed I had rice in my hair, I said, "I was just married this morning." "Where is your husband? She asked. "He is over there." And I pointed out to him, "Oh, no," and before I had time to react, she got up and walked over to Jimmy and told him to come over and sit down next to me.

That evening, after we registered at our hotel, we dined at the "Chalet Suizo" restaurant, Jimmy had visited them many times on his trips through Mexico City on his way to the States, for many years you couldn't make connection to the States the same day, so you had to wait until the next day flight. We asked for a small saucer at the restaurant as a souvenir, they were very happy to give it to us, I still have it. That night I gave Jimmy my virginity.

The next morning, I called my cousin Esperanza, on my father's side, she didn't take no for an answer, we had to go eat dinner with them that day. They wanted to meet Jimmy. Her husband Raul and their children, all in college. Lucila, Raul, Jaime, Lourdes and Car-lota, were on hand for the banquet. We had a wonderful dinner. I was happy Jimmy had met another part of my family.

Just going to the motion of leaving my family and my beloved country, I was numb, I was scared of what was coming ahead, that unknown subject that you can't see and only love makes you keep walking. I knew I couldn't live without Jimmy. I had to go with him. When the plane was taking off, Jimmy put his arm around me and told me, "Don't be afraid, baby, I will always love you, you are my life."

We left Mexico December 15, 1964. Since it was December, the city was all lit up; it was so beautiful from the air. Jimmy saw the tears in my eyes and held my hands and told me, "I will always love you, baby. We'll come to visit your mama, and she can come and visit as well. You'll see, you'll like living in the States."   And so, I left Mexico for the greatest adventure of my life.

Chapter Two

We arrived in Houston, Texas the same night, we went to a hotel close to the airport, Jimmy sat on the floor next to me, he said. "I want to talk to you about something, you know I want to go overseas, and women get together and talk about everything the men tell them about the job. I don't want you to do that, anything I tell you, it has to stay with you, if I hear it somewhere I know where it came from and I won't tell you anything again, is that understood? But I didn't understand, because if some of the other men's wives told, it didn't have to come from me, but I didn't know how to respond. So I only nodded my head.

The next day, we took a taxi and went to a car dealership, and Jimmy bought a car, I only remember it was a Chrysler, but don't remember any details other that it was white. The next day, we left for Kountze, to visit his parents, we spent the night there. They welcomed us with open arms, I remembered my mother-in-law specially. She took me to the living room while the men went outside to smoke a cigarette and drink a cup of coffee, we could hear their laughter, and she told me, "I know Teeny and you will be very happy because I know how much my son's loves you," she said, "I want to thank you for all you have left behind to be with Teeny." I was always grateful she talked to me like that.

The next day, he took me to meet his brother Corky, he always called him Cork. They were the closest of all, because they played together as children and fished together as adults. His name was Bert but no one called him by his name but his wife, her name was Adele; they were both very happy people. They barbequed that night, while Corky and Jimmy were outside cooking, drinking a beer and kidding each other, Adele and I were fixing the trimming for the barbeque, That was their specialty, I found out whenever they got together, there was a barbeque being prepared. We spent the next night there; they lived in Nederland, Texas, just South of Beaumont.

The next day we went to Hackberry, Louisiana, Jimmy's brother Jack, lived there with his wife Elmarie, they had two children, a son and a daughter, Allen Dale and Carol Ann. I had corresponded with Elmarie before my marriage to Jimmy because Elmarie and my mother-in-law had been trying to make arrangements over here for our Catholic wedding in Mexico. They were trying to get a Priest here to write a letter to my Priest in Mexico, that Jimmy had never been married in any church.

We spent the next night there, Elmarie was a very good cook, but Jack didn't barbeque, she told me, "If we get hungry for barbeque in this house, I do it in this house."

The only brother I hadn't met yet was Tyke, but he wrote to me many times, before we finally met.

Then, we left for Morgan City on the coast of Louisiana, in the Gulf of Mexico, lots of oil businesses were located there, the streets were narrow and there was a lot of traffic. I remembered it was raining, and I didn't like it, but Of course I didn't tell Jimmy. He said we would go to another town close by to look for an apartment. We spent the next night in Morgan City.

He check with his company the next morning, and off we went to Thibodaux, Louisiana. We found an apartment there. The apartment was furnished, but there were still many things we had to buy. We had our first home.

The rig was in the shipyard for repairs, Jimmy worked twelve hours on the rig and then ten hours at home, because traveling time. Morgan City wasn't very far from Thibodaux but it was out of town. He was tired when he came home so he would shower and go to bed, and then he was getting up just on time to eat something and go back to work. My days became extremely long. I started to get lonelier and lonelier. I would get a big box of Kleenex and go sit on the floor between two chairs and cry my eyes out. I didn't like being married like that.

Jimmy came home one night and saw me sitting on the floor crying, he was very upset, he had no idea what was going on with me. He started staying up longer with me and taking me out. He bought a television set and tried to make things nicer for me, after all, I didn't know anyone, I didn't have anyone to talk to, and that was not what I expected of a happy married life.

I started meeting people, going to church with one of my neighbors, her name was Alice Leblanc, she used to tell people we were sisters, because her family lived in Plaquemine, She didn't have family there either. Her husband name was Xavier, but everybody called him Xey, They had five daughters and Alice still found time to introduce me to her friends, all of the men worked evening shift, so we played cards at someone's house every night, we played for pennies, but we had a lot of fun. One night, they started telling each other what a bad time they had having their babies and one had a worse time than the other one. That night, the husband had not left for work yet, so he came over and leaned by the door and said, "anyone who would hear talk would think you were about to die." Without missing a beat, the lady who was telling the story, looked at him and asked him, "have you ever crapped a watermelon?" He left.

It was a lot better once the rig went to the Gulf because Jimmy was working one week, but then he was home one week.

Then we went to the Courthouse to get married so I could get my papers in order, but when we got to the Courthouse, Jimmy's birth certificate was "too old", they told Jimmy it couldn't be over ninety days old. Jimmy told them, "but I'm over ninety days old." The blood test we had brought from Louisiana wasn't accepted in Texas. It had to be done here in Texas. So we couldn't get married that week. My mother-in-law wrote to Dayton, where Jimmy was born and asked for his birth certificate. Jimmy went back to work.

When he came back from work and we came back to Texas to get married again, we got married that time. My mother-in-law baked a pineapple upside down cake for our wedding cake.

Then I had to go back to Mexico to get my papers in order to be able to stay in the United States as a permanent resident. But to accomplish that, I had to stay in Mexico six weeks without coming back to the States until my papers were ready. When I came back I was a resident.

I started to get sick and Alice took me to her Doctor, I was pregnant, I was due in November, Jimmy and I were both very happy.

Right about that time, my father-in-law started to get very sick; He was diagnosed with lung cancer. We traveled to Texas the next day after Jimmy came home from the rig. I stayed back in Texas to help out. We did that for several months.

Then the contract ran out for Jimmy's rig, and Jimmy was going to be without a job again, so he went to New Orleans with some of the other men from the rig to try to get a job elsewhere. The company they visited was sending a full crew to England. Jimmy's father was worse but Jimmy couldn't stay without a job, as hard as it was for him, he decided we had to leave.

When I called home and told my mother where we were going, she said, "You see? That's why I didn't want you to marry Jimmy, how are we going to tell your Grandmother you are going to England?" Well, when they did tell her, they said she looked at them and said, "I'm glad to know one of my Granddaughters is going to see the world."

By that time I was seven months pregnant. We were to fly out of Houston because we were going to visit Jimmy's Dad before we left. He was very bad off. Then we flew to New York, there, we met with the rest of the company who were also going to England. From there to London, the weather was so bad; we had to be transferred to another airport in New Jersey because they had closed the New York airport. From there, we flew to London, when we were close to London, we were awaken by a loud bell, breakfast, breakfast, I looked at my watch and asked them, "at three o'clock in the morning?" The stewardess answered, it's nine in the morning in London.

It was the longest trip of my life. Everybody was talking about how tired they were, with my pregnancy, I was so tired, I couldn't even tell anyone how tired I was. London was only a stopover, but the weather was so bad, they had stopped all flights out of London, we were to fly out to Scarborough, Yorkshire. It was October 1965 and winter had set in England; it was for me, anyway. After all, before now, winter was only a word to me; I had never been anywhere where it was that cold.

All flights had been cancelled in London to go anywhere, but they wouldn't let us go find a hotel, they would say we had to wait thirty minutes, at a time, until it became several hours. The men and some of the women, spent their time in the bar, which was open for two hours at a time, and then they would announce the last order for a drink, until they reopened the bar again. I guess that keeps people from getting drunk.

I tried to lay down on one of the benches at the airport, but with not even a pillow, it was very hard getting comfortable with my big stomach. I was so sick, and Jimmy was so mad; he told the airline they could do whatever they wanted to, but he was taking me to a hotel. The fact that we changed airlines there, no one was responsible for anybody. That's when they decided they had a plane ready for us.

They flew us to an airport in the middle of nowhere, there; they put us in a bus and were driven for hours to Scarborough, Yorkshire. I dragged myself out, with Jimmy's help, of course, the Company had rented a Villa exclusively for us, when we all got into our room, we found ourselves waiting in line to use the bathroom, rooms didn't have a bathroom. It's kind of funny now, but no one was laughing then.

British customs are really different, we watched them set the tables for the next day breakfast, we thought they were decorating the tables with these beautiful ornaments, when we looked closer, we found out there were putting the toasts on the table for the next day breakfast, the night before.

One day, I had a headache. So Jimmy said, let's go buy some aspirins, we need to have some on hand anyway, so we went to the drugstore, he ordered, "may I have Bayer aspirins, please?" the lady brought a small bottle of off-brand aspirins. Jimmy asked again. "May I have Bayer aspirins, please?" The lady came back with a bigger bottle of the same off brand aspirins. So Jimmy again asked "Don't you have Bayer aspirins?" to which she replied, "I thought you were asking for a bigger size." We laughed about that all the way to the Villa and years after.

There were two old British Ladies living at the Villa, I was visiting with them, one of the men, who was from Louisiana, kept coming with stories to the Ladies about Louisiana, she would looked at him and would not say anything, finally, the man asked this Lady, "Do you think I chop up English a lot, do you?" To which she replied, "Sir, I don't think you speak English, at all." (This story it's important to me because being from Mexico, my English is criticized a lot by some Americans. Yet, my English was accepted in England better than the American English.) Perhaps because in Europe, most people speak several languages, and are used to an accent from a different language.

We found a beautiful house in Filey, a small community just outside of Scarborough, we only had our luggage, but it was good because the house was fully furnished. Two stories, I wasn't crazy about that, but most houses were two stories, they said because there is not a lot of land.

As soon as we moved in and bought a few groceries, Jimmy and I started to cook our very first meal, in the middle of our cooking creation, the gas went out, so I went just around the back of the house to Thelma's to let her know we were out of gas and needed to be reported. Thelma smiled and said, "No, we only need to put some shillings in the meter." "What meter?" I asked her.

"The one in the utility closet." "Come on," she said, "I show you." We went back to our place, and she put a few shillings in the meter and sure enough, the fire came back on again. She said, we leased the house by the week, during the summer time. That's the only way we can get the utilities paid up by our renters. The electricity used to run on a meter as well, that one was run by pennies, but we had it changed before you moved in." she told me.

I started having problems with my pregnancy; Jimmy took me to a doctor someone recommended to him. She was a very nice old lady doctor. She put me in the hospital, mainly because she didn't want me to stay alone every day so close to my due date, and not even a phone anywhere. She said I was exhausted with the trip and I needed to rest.

The rig was in the shipyard, North of Scarborough, all the men traveled to the rig every day, left home at 6:00 a.m. they were back about 7:00 p.m. It was hard on everybody.

I was in the hospital two weeks before I went into labor, I remember one morning one of the nurses opened the drapes, and for the first time in my life, I saw snow! I was so happy, I told every nurse who came into my room, how beautiful everything looked. "Mrs. Moore, you don't mean that!" "Yes, I do, I think it looks beautiful."

"Well, it doesn't look pretty when you have to go to work on a moped with snow everywhere."

The doctor didn't want me to have the baby then, because it was early, when I started having pains, it wasn't in the abdomen like most women have, my pains were on my low back, I thought it was my kidneys, I had just eaten a big pear, and I said, is not labor pains, it's the pear. I was eight month and one week pregnant, the Doctor said that babies gain most of their weight the ninth month, the baby was coming twisted and every time they tried to straighten him out, he would go back to the original position, the doctor recommended a C-Section, all of this happened at night, but Jimmy had not left the hospital yet. So he was stop on time, before he left the building. I remember when they wheeled me into the elevator on the way to the operating room, one of the nurses said to me. "Good bye Mrs. Moore." "Oh," I said crying, "don't tell me good bye." I was so scared, I thought she was telling me good bye for good. It was a boy; he was born at 12:05 a.m. on the 10th of November 1965. We named him James Merle, James for his father, Merle for his Grandfather. When the women saw me again, they asked me, "Mrs. Moore, how is the pear?"

I stayed in the hospital two more weeks because I was alone so much, and because we lived in a two story house. While I was in the hospital, Jimmy's Dad died, he tried to come back to the States for the funeral, but all the airports were closed, in England and in the United States. The doctor told me, "I don't want to appear unkind, but I didn't want your husband to leave with you in the hospital, he said he'll be back on time to take you home, but what about if something happens to him in this weather? No, I'm glad the airports were closed."

After I came home, they sent a nurse to check on me every day. The neighbors, who didn't know me at all. Would come in and after they introduced themselves, they rolled their sleeves and washed diapers, (there were no disposable diapers at that time) or wash dishes or whatever they could see that needed to be done. They would also do my shopping, or fix me something to eat. Anyone who says British people are unfriendly has not lived in England. They are some of the warmest people I have ever known.

While in the hospital, Jimmy and I befriended a younger couple whom she lost their baby, but they had a beautiful little girl, Rachel, about three years old, Elspeth and Keith Taylor. Jimmy and Keith got to be friends sooner because while I was in the hospital, when Keith found out where Jimmy lived, he told Jimmy he had to come by our house any way on his way to the hospital, so he started picking Jimmy up every night.

We visited with them the whole time we lived in England. When we returned home we wanted to see them again but had no way to contact them. So we decided to surprise them with a visit, when we arrived, they were happy but very surprised with the unexpected visit then, but at first, when they didn't know we would come to visit them without any notice. "Over here, they said later on, we send a postcard giving people a fortnight notice." "What is a fortnight?" I asked. "That is two weeks' notice that you are going to visit." "My God," I said, "why didn't you let us know?" "Well, at first, we didn't know how to tell you, and then we began to like it, we could also visit you without notice, now, (she told me years later) Thelma and I do the same. Thelma and Brian were our landlords, also became very friendly with them. That's how Keith and Elsepth and Thelma met.

We went out for dinner almost every time Jimmy was in town. Jimmy and I always had good memories of them.

We also, befriended our next door neighbors and landlords, they were Brian and Thelma Wright, they had twin girls, Debbie and Julie, and also enjoyed their company, Thelma's mother was one of the ladies who came in to help me after the baby was born.

Jimmy would carry the baby downstairs before 6:00 a.m. to help me. Because he had to be ready to be picked up at 6:00 a.m. he would come home by 7:00 p.m. every day, including weekends. The baby seemed to know when his Dad was coming home, as little as he was, he would be restless until Daddy came in and held him in his arms.

I would hold the baby in my arms for hours while he slept, it was so cold in the house, we had a fireplace, but that was the only heat we had, and all the houses were the same. Jimmy put a big tub and fill it up to the top with charcoal every day for the fireplace, I remember when they showed us the house, they said, "this is the coal room." I said, "The whole house its cold." Thelma responded, "No, coal for the fireplace."

I would burn the whole tub of coals in one day. A truck would come and dump coal in that little room. Later on in the day, Thelma would come to my house to warm up because she told me, I don't light up the fireplace until the twins and Keith come home." They said it was the worst winter they had in thirty years. And I had to be there.

We had ice inside of the windows; of course I had never seen anything like it. People said from the road everybody knew where the Americans lived, because our roof didn't have nearly as much ice as the rest of the houses. Our entrance was steep, we used the side entrance and come in from the kitchen, but the mailman had to come from the front of the house, and he had to crawl to climb the steep entrance, because of the ice.

I remember asking Jimmy, "Do you love me?" he would quickly respond, "if I didn't love you, would I let you put your cold feet on my legs?"

One day, he had to go to Sunderland, on a business trip with some of the people from the company, as he entered the restaurant, Harley Miller, his friend from Coatzacoalcos, my hometown, was sitting there eating dinner! What a surprise.

One day, Jimmy came home with several of his buddies from work. Some were more drunk than others. Jimmy and this other guy were rocking on the door frame telling each other which one of the two loves their wife the most. Finally the other guy told Jimmy, you don't love your wife more than I love mine, she just have you domesticated. You prefer to stay with her than to go with us to play cards. Jimmy told him, if I prefer you to her, then I'm in trouble buddy. All the guys laughed and left, leaving Jimmy alone.

The New Years came; Jimmy came home from work one day and gave me a letter, he said, "I'm sorry but I don't know what to say." The letter was in English, address to Jimmy so he would be able to let me know, my Grandmother had passed away, they didn't want me to know before Christmas, she had died, October 31, they thought it was best to wait until after the New Year. There is no good time for bad news. She had died two weeks before Jimmy's Dad.

Finally spring time came, I could push little Jimmy in his pram, because I had to walk every-where I went, we had a car but it was parked while Jimmy was gone. I didn't drive. But since they drive on the wrong side of the road, I elected to walk. When Jimmy was gone, Keith and Elspeth would come over to take me to their home for tea whenever they could. They understood very well how lonely I was even when I never said anything.

I wanted to have little Jimmy baptized, the Godparents were my sister Reyna Violeta and her husband, we could do it by proxy, Mrs. Audrey Dugas's oldest son and daughter would stand as Godparents. Mr. Dugas worked on the opposite crew from Jimmy but we knew them very well. As Catholics we don't like to wait until the person is grown. We had Jimmy baptized and then a small reception at home.

Summer was a lot of fun, the population in Filey tripled, this was a tourist town and their industry depended solely on tourism, you also had to watch for bicyclers, they were fast and plenty of them. We were right on the coastline, so we had beaches, people would wear overcoats to the beach, I'm sure because of the bad winter we had suffered that year. Other people went to swimming pools, people had to wait in line to get in the pool, there were so many people.

Restaurants were great, always had very interesting things to see around the pub, they displayed lots of antiques. Jimmy always wanted a steak so we went to restaurants that offered that kind of menu. One of the dishes I enjoyed was Yorkshire pudding, served with roast beef and gravy. Elspeth taught me that, she invited us for dinner one night and had Yorkshire pudding and roast beef, it was delicious. That dish is typical of Yorkshire, where we lived.

That summer Scarborough celebrated 2000 years since the Vikings left England, a marching band Parade of bagpipe players, all with their Scottish kilts were beautiful in blue and white, I love the bagpipes. A lot of people don't care for them, but when you see a Parade of at least 50 men in a marching band, the sound is great. If you don't have that, the effect is diminished. I had always felt very lucky I was there at that parade. It was a beautiful celebration.

That summer, Jimmy and I took long drives when he was home, everything was new to us so we look in the map and decide which direction we wanted to go that day. We went to Whitby Abbey, is still hard to comprehend something like that was built in the year 657. The first establishment at Whitby was a double monastery for men and women which formed a marked feature of the early Anglo-Saxon Church and was presided over the Abbess. (This information I took from the booklet I brought from the Abbey when we visited there.)

We went to the Petrified Forrest, where hundreds of giant trees were laying on the ground, and the trees had been there for hundreds of years, were all petrified. It's a weary feeling the first time you see it.

The castles were one of my favorite things to see in England, there are just about everywhere, you're driving along and make a turn somewhere, and there is a castle, many times over. When you come from somewhere and are not used to see castles. This is when you go on a vacation.

Also, we went to a town called, Nottingham, and there is a Museum dedicated to the Robin Hood Legend, the Shires of Sherwood and Saxon still exists, there is all kind of memorabilia about Robin Hood, King Richard and the Sheriff of Nottingham. If Robin Hood didn't exist, you can't tell by the Museum in his honor, it was neat just being there and reading all about it.

We had to go to Liverpool to get the baby's passport, we went by train, we changed trains in Manchester, and then we went to Liverpool, hometown of the Beetles that was fun. It took all day, but it was across the country so that wasn't bad when you look at it that way. When we arrived at the American Embassy, we had to have the baby's measurements, I knew his weight but when they asked how tall he was, Jimmy stretched his arm out and touching his elbow, he said, "this long." The ladies at the Embassy laughed and said they had never been given measurements in that manner.

One of the ladies from the company took care of the baby while Jimmy and I went to Liverpool, I took so many clothes and diapers for the baby, and his pram was full. When we return, I found out I had forgotten to bring his milk!

This lady was only one of three who had babies while we were in England; they got pregnant after we arrived there. They used to say that it was the cold weather that did it.

One of the trips that have stayed in my mind is when we went to Scotland that summer. They have many castles and some of them are used as hotels, for us, it was so elegant just to be able to stay there. It was like going to the movies, only you are playing in it. All the staff was dressed in gothic costumes, which added to the charm. Edinburgh it's a beautiful city. We went by train. Traveling by train was customary in Europe; trains are fast and very comfortable. Also, Jimmy could enjoy the scenery. The only thing, In Europe, they rather you bring your dog than your child. Never the less, we enjoy ourselves.

Little Jimmy's birthday was coming up, and I wanted to make a piñata for his birthday. We used a clay pot as a base in Mexico;

of course there was not one in all of England. I finally decided to buy a glass fish bowl. I made a star with all colors of paper I could find, finally the birthday came, friends and neighbors came curious to see what a piñata looked like, They loved it, but it couldn't be broken because it was glass, so the candy I previously had put in, I just swung the piñata, then I reached in and threw the candies on the floor for the kids to picked up, even adults were picking up the candies. It was a lot of fun.

The next morning, my neighbors' twin girls came over telling me they had told everyone at school about the birthday party they had gone to and that we had a piñata. So everybody in school wanted to see the piñata, they asked if they could take it with them to school. Of course they could. They said the piñata was displayed in all the class rooms for everyone to see. I was proud my creation had brought so much pleasure to so many people. If my memory serves me correctly I gave them the piñata to keep.

Blanca with the piñata she made in England

After that, the rig was sent to Norway, but the families stayed in England. Jimmy started working twenty days on and twenty days off. It was very nice when Jimmy was home for one month, but then he had to leave and that part was always very hard. One of the women said: "I like it better when Charlie works five and three, it took Charlie one day to get home, so to me, was seven and one, that's just the way I like it."

One day, Jimmy invited a man from the rig, and his family for dinner, then he proceeded to cook Chili con Carne, and a pot of beans. It seems they had a heated conversation about who could eat hotter food, Jimmy was cooking to stop his friend from telling him he could eat hotter than he could, unaware of his little plan, I tasted the food, and tears rolled down my face! No one is going to be able to eat, I thought. I knew the best cure for hot food is sugar, so I put plenty of sugar in Jimmy's dinner. He didn't know what had happened to his dinner. I explained to him I had put sugar in the food, I didn't know about the plan, but women and children were eating dinner too. We all had a good laugh.

We were in England eighteen months, at the end of the summer we were leaving, the company offered Jimmy to stay on, but the North Sea is very dangerous, so he elected to go elsewhere. We had to sell our car; the neighbor told me of a gardener of some man who came to park his Bentley behind our house, where there were special parking garages for people who didn't have the space at home. I waited for the man, he went in and couldn't start his car, so he was leaving by foot, I went out and spoke to him about our little Austin Prince, it was an old car, but it ran beautifully, Jimmy made the remark several times about "he wish he could bring that old car to the States because it was so reliable."

So I explained to the man about how reliable our car was "it start every time," I told him, then I notice he had this strange look in his face, after all, he owned a Bentley, I said, "Oh, I'm not offering you my car, it's for your gardener. Could you please ask him to come?" He smiled and said. "Yes, Madam, I'll tell him to talk to you about your car." Jimmy laughed about that every time he thought about it. He said he could just imagine the man thinking what is this crazy woman doing?

We left England and came back to the States through Spain, we went to Madrid. We toured several cities, but his favorite was always Toledo. He loved being there, and so did I. When we arrived in Toledo, Jimmy asked a guard at the entrance of a restaurant to guide us to a Museum, "There is no Museum in Toledo Sir, Toledo is a Museum." He told Jimmy, and we toured every inch of it, Jimmy was always kin of swords and knives made in Toledo Spain, now he was there to see them first hand. They took us to a factory where they were made.

Then we flew to Houston, his brother Robert and his new bride Iris, met us at the airport, the next day, they were going to the store and wanted to take little Jimmy with them, I ran out of the door with a sweater, Robert said, "No, he doesn't need a sweater here." It was July.

We went to Kountze, Jimmy was very happy to see his family, of course, then he called the company he had worked for before in Morgan City, Zapata off- shore, and asked if they had anything over-seas, they did, I thought the floor would swallow me when Jimmy asked me, "how do you like to go to Australia?" Of course, he knew I would go to the end of the earth with him, I told him that once, now it became true.

We went to Nederland to visit his brother Corky and Adele. Corky had been preparing barbeque, so they both stayed outside cooking, I went inside to visit with Adele, we could hear them teasing each other and laughing all the way into the house, they always loved to barbeque, cooking it and drinking a beer it was part of the ritual. They had a lot of fun doing that.

The next morning we packed to go visit with Jack and Elmarie, and he was ready to pack to go to Australia. "You may want to leave," I said, "but I'm going to Mexico." He couldn't believe he had forgotten I hadn't been home to see my family! He also had his son, Earl to come visit with us. Jimmy took him fishing. Jimmy always loved to fish.

I remember someone from the Zapata's office went to the airport when we were on our way to Mexico, to pick up Jimmy's passport so they could get his papers ready to go to Australia. At that time, he could travel to Mexico with only his driver's license. Also, we found out to go to Australia, he had to go ahead for thirty days by himself and then I could go, because a lot of people would make the trip and then wouldn't stay.

So we went to Mexico City for a few days, visited with my sister and her family, she has three sons and one daughter, Miguel, Luis, Patricia and the youngest one its Francisco, named after our Dad. They were on their way to college.

We also visited with all of my daddy's family, there were still two surviving sisters, Amparo and her children, Socorro, Esperanza (Jimmy met her when we got married), and Ignacio. We also visited with my uncle Marcelo and my Aunt Blanca. I inherited my name from her. They had three grown children, Julio, Sergio and Amalia. Since they were both retired they wanted us to stay with them but time was precious to us, we haven't been to see my mother yet.

Coatzacoalcos was so hot, my son Jimmy opened the refrigerator door and lay down in it; we missed him and found him lying down in the fridge. We were all very upset by it and he didn't understand it, after all, he had found the coolest place in the house. And after we visit with my Aunts and my cousins and their families we went back to Mexico City. It was a lot better when we went back to Mexico City; it was warm during the day time but cool at night.

We brought my mama with us to the U.S. because I didn't want to stay any longer in Mexico since Jimmy had to leave so soon to go to Australia. It was winter in Australia, so we went winter shopping in the summer, that was difficult, but we managed to find some wool shirts and other items. And so, Jimmy left to go to Melbourne, Victoria.

He liked Australia a lot, he found an apartment in Frankston, and so we wouldn't be living in such big city. It was so peaceful there he liked it better.

My mama, little Jimmy and I stayed in Kountze at my mother-in-law's house. It was surprising how she and my mother could communicate, but they did. We made a couple of trips to Beaumont, shopping and lunch. It was my mother's first trip to United States so she didn't want to miss anything. My mother and Adele loved to shop so they usually would stay behind together because they would look at every little thing from every angle.

I had to go to Zapata's Houston's office to get my papers ready and my tickets, they told me there were complications with my papers because I had Mexican Passport and they were not familiar with what all that was involved, Mexico didn't have as many embassies all over the world like the U.S. did.

Then, the time came for little Jimmy and I to go to Australia, and we left for Melbourne. My mother's flight was later than mine, so my mother-in-law took her to her terminal. After my flight had left.

We stopped in Honolulu for two days to break the long trip to Melbourne, little Jimmy and I took several tours in Honolulu, we enjoyed it. Then we flew to Australia. I thought we were never going to get there. They gave little Jimmy a certificate for crossing the International Date Line. And everybody else got hot towels for our faces and arms; it was very soothing on a flight that long. The flight was not crowded, so I could arrange two seats to fix little Jimmy a bed. I think we landed on every island in the Pacific.

We finally arrived in Melbourne; Jimmy was at the airport waiting for us, so happy to see each other and our son. The drive to Frankston, seems that it was about one hour from Melbourne, I was happy that Jimmy thought that Frankston, was a better place to live for little Jimmy. While I couldn't stay awake, little Jimmy was wide awake and ready to play with Daddy. I slept about 15 hours when Jimmy finally thought I had enough sleep and woke me up; he had a roast ready for supper. I took a quick cold shower to help me wake up and visit with my family.

The next day Jimmy drove us to Melbourne to meet some of the people from the company at their already acquired Pub, since I had the baby with me, I just sat on the outside of the entrance door. Everybody was drinking and smoking, I didn't like that atmosphere.

Jimmy had good friend, Larry, who worked on the same rig but for different company, Jimmy invited him for dinner the following

Saturday, time came for him to arrive, a couple of hours later and Larry hadn't shown up, we didn't have a phone, at that time, some private homes didn't have one, at least not in an apartment, so he couldn't call us. Two hours later, he showed up, but we had gone ahead and ate. He said he had this guy with him he couldn't get rid of, and he didn't want to just not show up, he had told him he had a dinner engagement, when he told him he had been invited for dinner at James Moore's home, nothing to do but bring him along, so he did. Not that he was a good friend of Jimmy, they only knew each other from working together on a rig every once in a while.

The man was so inebriated he could hardly speak, but managed to ask where a bed w as. I looked at Jimmy. Jimmy stood up and told him, "come on; I'll take you." And closed the door on him. Larry apologized, but guaranteed us we'd rather that he is sleep on our bed than be out here with us. I said, "Yes, I just didn't plan to change the bed again tonight."

The drunken man left the next day to go back to the States with his wife, several months later, he came back to Australia by himself, we were in Perth by then, he and his wife were divorced, she had shot him in the stomach, he was so proud she shot him five times and didn't kill him. He said the doctor told him she used a 22 caliber and didn't go through the several layers of fat he had in his stomach. He would show the scars to anyone who would look, he was very proud of the scars. The reason I had to include this story is because Jimmy thought it was so funny and for many years he laughed about it every time he remembered it.

We met a young couple, Jimmy and Pete worked together and he brought his wife Christy with him, a young woman from Wales, she was a charming young woman, we immediately liked each other, they were in their late twenties, and Jimmy and Pete really got along well. We saw each other often while we lived in Frankston.

There was another couple that came over to visit with us, Carl and Bobbie, Carl and Jimmy were good friends from the rig, he and his wife were close to Jimmy's age, so they would tease Jimmy about me, "What do you want with an old guy like Jim?" and I would tell him. "Because he is who I want." "Do you? Really?" I would get so mad that they thought it was funny. Jimmy would tell me, don't pay them any mind Baby, they just want to play with you. But I didn't see the humor in it.

We were in the Melbourne area only four months, enough time to tour museums, the Zoo and the botanical gardens. We also went to a place where Captain Cook landed, and they had shows to re-live Captain Cook's landing. Also they have Aborigines performing dances and bow and arrows exhibitions and of course boomerang demonstrations and displays, and sales of all kind of souvenirs for the many tourists. We brought lots of boomerangs for the family, we enjoyed it all.

We were off to Perth, Western Australia. Eight hours flight with-out stopping. Jimmy had to ride the rig to location in the North part of Western Australia that was why we were moved to Perth.

So little Jimmy and I made the trip by ourselves, we checked into our hotel and started looking for a house, I found a house in a very neat neighborhood, Attadale. It was furnished, so I was able to move in before Jimmy got back from the rig. He was really pleased when he saw the house. Our neighbors could not have been nicer. They all came to introduce themselves and offered whatever we needed so we could get ourselves settled.

Our house was only about five blocks from the Swan River; it was wonderful to see the black swans swimming with their little babies. Of course we have never seen black swans since there are very few places they can be found in the world. The whole time we lived in Perth, our favorite ride was to go to the Swan River, and just walk by the river and feed the swans and their young ones.

One day, Jimmy came from the office and told me he had heard the rig he was on in England sank in the rough waters of the North Sea, didn't know about casualties, my legs got weak, I sat on the nearest chair, my God, what if Jimmy had been on it! Many of the men on the rig Jimmy knew and he felt very bad about it. Jimmy was never able to obtain a list of the casualties.

We lived about five miles from Fremantle, one of Australia's most important Ports. I loved to go shopping there, also, it was an area where you can find, Greek, Italian, Indian and Spanish among other races and their shops. So, you can find a great variety of their merchandise in the same area. That was my favorite place to eat, different kinds of foods, the ingredients, and the restaurants.

Jimmy, young Jimmy and I, went for long rides, sometimes we went for a few days out of town, we went to Pemberton, on the South of Perth, where the biggest tree was registered. The Karri Eucalyptus – Diversicolor tree, the one we saw had a plate with the dimensions as follows:

Girth at 4' ft. 3"	19 ft. 5"
height to first limb	158 ft.
total height	265 ft.
volume	2350 cu. Ft.

And it's unbelievable tall.

On the way to Pemberton, we would stop along the road just to rest a little and walk to the water, it was the Indian Ocean, which we could see from the road, and a huge rainbow was forming out of the water. We watched it for a long time. We had left the camera in the car so Jimmy rushed to the car to get the camera; by the time he came back the rainbow had disappeared. But the image of it always stayed with us. On those occasions Jimmy would tell me, "Baby, we don't have a picture but no one can take away the image from our mind."

From there we went to Albany, in the south western Australia, a tourist town; they have a natural stone bridge we walked over the bridge, it's a neat feeling when you are walking on it, they also a rock that has a figure of a dog's head among their local attractions. We visited a whale station, it was 1967, so there were new laws that didn't allow fishermen to kill whales any longer, there were still a few men there hanging around the whale station, they fished for whales all their lives and now they felt their live hood has been taken away from them. Albany had a big fishing industry besides tourism, and the whale station was empty until they heard whether they could catch any more whales. We bought several whale teeth; Jimmy liked to work with his hands, and wanted them for gun handles.

There were so many things to see in Perth, everything was new to us, so we really went all the time, because little Jimmy didn't have to go to school yet.

There was sort of a safari park north of Perth, the kind that you drive in and the animals are lose, there were lions that would jump on your car sometimes, but they had a truck with red meat and they fed the lions. We were ordered to keep our windows up, not that they needed to give the order, In 1967 that was a big attraction. They also had different signs like, "trespassers will be eaten." And others, just as comical as that one. We took many pictures of the lions eating on the hood of our car.

Then there was the Kings park, it's a huge park where you can take a picnic lunch and relax, or jog around the park, or drive around it, it was at the highest point of Perth, and you could see the whole city from the top. On the way out there was a Wind Mill, you could go in and tour it and buy souvenirs in it.

Jimmy had to go to Singapore for a while; it wouldn't be for too long, so little Jimmy and I stayed in Perth, after about one month, Jimmy called me one day and asked me if we could be ready to go back to the States in ten days. I had a small child, two dogs, one car to sell and a whole house to pack, in ten days, was he kidding me? The Lord was with me, He always has been. When the ten days were due, there was no plane out of Singapore to Perth. So the help Jimmy was going to offer was to take the luggage to the car, and he wasn't there! So I moved us to a hotel, sent the dogs ahead, and cleaned the house before I moved out. When Jimmy came, he showed me his manicured hands; I showed him all my broken finger nails. We laughed about that several times.

Our two years in Australia were up and it was time to plan to come back to the United States. Our neighbors got together and gave us a going away party, I was so surprised, it was very sweet. And everyone was there with a regular banquet and gifts to see us off. We were staying at the hotel a couple of days to rest before we started our long journey home.

Chapter Three

Vacation time for everybody, we just went everywhere, Jimmy tried to get his son Earl to come to visit, but his mother always had an excuse not to let him come, it didn't matter to her that it had been two years since Jimmy has seen his son. She would give an excuse like, he had to baby sit his younger siblings. Jimmy would drive to Houston to pick Earl up and she would only give him permission for one or two days. That was after father and son had not seen each other for two years. This always affected Jimmy, he was distraught by it.

I suggested to Jimmy that he should fight for his son in court; he had enough reasons to have his son with him. He would say "No, it would be a mess and he didn't and Earl to find out a lot of things that would have to come out in court." I said "but he will find out sometime." Jimmy would say. "Yes, but not in court, and not by me."

I did go to Mexico for my trip home, Jimmy always went with me, we visited all my family, go to Museums, night clubs and restaurants', visiting the Pyramids of the Sun and the Moon in Teotihuacán, Northeast of Mexico City was one of our favorite trips.

My mother told me she was going to give me my father's Visa when he came to the United States as a youngster to go to school, when I read the paper, I couldn't believe my eyes, my father entered the United States on the day Jimmy was born, day and year. A coincidence? I had always considered it fate. My father was 23 years old at that time.

Again, it was time to call the office and find out where they wanted Jimmy to go next. It was Singapore. We planned to go together, but again my Mexican Passport prevented me from traveling with my husband, we were all packed, when we received a phone call from the office letting him know they could not obtain a visa for me, they had everything ready for him and little Jimmy, Jimmy said. "Wait a minute, I can't take my son with me, he has to stay with his mother."

So, we had to wait thirty extra days before we could leave.

When it was time for little Jimmy and I to leave, we went via San Francisco – Tokyo – Hong Kong and then landed in Singapore. With a layover in Honolulu, Jimmy wanted us to rest on the way.

When Jimmy met us at the airport, little Jimmy couldn't speak very well yet, but he could make himself understand, he asked his Daddy, "This is where you were hiding." Jimmy answered him, "Yes, but you found me."

Jimmy had an apartment ready for us, and we moved in. We had a big yard, and only one neighbor upstairs, it was an Australian couple, Jimmy came home one day with Pete and Christy, the couple we had met in Frankston, I was so happy to see them. They had a son now, and she was expecting another child, we made a foursome often and have dinner together, one day she found out Pete was sick and he was being moved to Djakarta, so the office asked Christy if she wanted to go they would make the arrangements for her to fly to Indonesia. She was so happy she was going to get to see Pete sooner, while she was at the airport, she was notified not to get on the plane, and she couldn't go. Pete had died, Pete had a case of appendicitis, but when you are on a drilling rig and can't be taken care of, it can be dangerous, we heard he was asked to go to town, he decided it was nothing but upset stomach, so he didn't want to leave, when he decided it was serious enough to leave the job, the sea was so rough they couldn't put a crew boat close enough to load Pete, a helicopter couldn't land on the rig either, by the time they got Pete off the rig, there was no time to do surgery. He died on the way to Djakarta.

We thought Christy was going to go crazy, she was asked what kind of funeral she wanted for Pete, asked if she wanted to have him cremated, that is the norm in Australia, so Pete was cremated, I went to the service, but I could not get close to Christy, she was devastated, also, she was expecting a baby. She decided to take Pete's ashes with her. All instructions were given for her trip, no one was to bother her about the urn with Pete's ashes, but later we heard when she was changing planes in Rome, as she was changing airlines, they insisted in opening the urn, Christy went to pieces, they investigated further and found out the contents of the urn and let them pass with her, untouched. I tried to get in touch with Christy several times. She never replied.

We were in Singapore a few months, when Jimmy had to ride the rig to Australia. Little Jimmy and I once again, traveled by ourselves to Sydney, Australia. We found a house in the community of St. Ives, a beautiful place with a three level garden, spacious living and dining room area, we loved the house. The Master bedroom was at the entrance and Jimmy's bedroom was at the end of the hall, because it was such a big house, I didn't want him to be scared sleeping out there by himself, so I asked him. "Do you want to sleep with Mommy tonight?" He responded, "Do I have a bedroom?" I said, "of course you do." "Let's go," there were two bedrooms side by side, "which one is my bedroom?" he said. He never wanted to sleep with Mama and Daddy, he was always very independent.

We had decided to sell the dog in the States so they wouldn't put him in quarantine, we bought Jimmy another small Australian silky terrier and the dog slept with Jimmy even when he wasn't allowed to, the dog would be under the bed, I would put Jimmy to bed and could hear Jimmy calling the dog after I walked out of his bedroom; he patted on the bed and said, "here dinkum."

I was feeling so sick of my stomach, I had to go the doctor, and I thought it was food poisoning; the doctor took samples for a blood test, the next day, I received a phone call from the doctor's office,

"Mrs. Moore. You have tested positive." I said, "Positive for what?" the voice said. "You are pregnant."

It had been almost three years since the birth of our son Jimmy, I was losing hope I would ever have another baby. I was so happy, I didn't tell anyone of my good news, some of the other women did tell, and their husband found out of the new baby through someone else.

I bought a beautiful musical koala bear for our new baby; it played "Waltzing Matilda" they claimed as the Australian hymn. I felt it was going to be a girl. So when Jimmy came home, I showed him the koala bear and told him, "This is for Lois." He was very happy. But he couldn't understand why I wanted another child with the problems I had when Jimmy was born. "Well," I said, "that was a longtime ago, I forgotten all about it, we have to give Jimmy a sister or a brother." But I knew in my heart, it was going to be a sister.

My friends couldn't believe I never told anyone I was pregnant, I said, "well, I learnt when you told and your husband found out of your pregnancy from one of the men from the rig. I wanted to be the one to tell Jimmy he was going to be a father again."

I had to stop drinking coffee because it made me so sick of my stomach and I stop cooking because I was so sick, but little Jimmy loved his bacon, so I fried his bacon, when I put it on the table with scramble eggs, he looked at it and asked, "who spit on my bacon?" "No one spit on your bacon son, I fried it, it is the heat." I said. "Okay." He said, and he was content to eat it.

While in Sydney, we visited the Opera House, you could go across the famous and beautiful Sydney Bridge and it would lead you to the Opera House still under construction, we would walk around where we were able to because of the construction, but we go inside sometimes. Outdoor was almost finished.

We took many trips to the city, we could go to Manly, a city across the Bay from Sydney, it was a beautiful trip and I loved to take the hydrofoil from there to Sydney, every opportunity I had. From there you could walk to town. There was a restaurant we loved to go to, they called it "The Square Building", which happened to be round, on the top of the building, it was the best restaurant and bar, it rotated but some people couldn't stand the rotation so there was a part that was immobile. We always went to the rotating part. You have a panoramic view of the whole city, quite a sight. It was 1968.

I met a lady from Mexico City, married to an Australian man, Keith and Conchita Lewis, she told me when she got married she was over thirty years old, she used to be a dancer for the Mexican ballet, and people used to ask her all the time when she was getting married, so one day, she told them. "I have an Australian boyfriend, as soon as he comes back, we'll get married." She said within a couple of months, she met her husband to be, and he proposed to her and within weeks, they got married and left for Australia." They all believed her story was true, although she tried to tell them it was her imagination working full time.

We went to Canberra, Australia's Capital; we had to go to the American Embassy for some papers. We went to the Snowy Mountains, rented a cabin and stayed a few days to do some trout fishing in a lake not far from Canberra, it was snowing very hard, Jimmy drove as far as he could but the road was closed. We were told the road opens very seldom during the summer and it was late September, so their winter was just over. To see so much snow, piles of the stuff everywhere. I was so sick of my stomach in the mountains.

We left for Singapore after only four months in Sydney. And we were in Singapore only four months that time, then I had to leave, so the airline would let me in the plane, after seven months, no pregnant woman can fly, but Jimmy wanted me to have our next child in the United States and I was due when time for us to come back to the States, if I didn't comeback, that would had made us stay in Singapore for our vacation.

While we were there, all I did was try to stay cool, we had an apartment with no central air, but two window air conditioners in each bedroom, then I ran the fans in the living room and dining room, it cooled the whole apartment, one of the ladies asked me "Don't you know how high electricity is in Singapore?" I said "Yes, but I don't drink or smoke, so at least, I can be cool."

Something I found interesting is that in Singapore, Television Stations offer the news in six languages, Chinese is the first language, perhaps because they outnumber everyone else, then there were news in Mandarin and Cantonese, both Chinese dialects, Hindu, Malay and English.

The only thing I could do in Singapore that time, was ride a taxi across to downtown to a coffee shop and drink Cappuccino coffee and a piece of their delicious cakes, I would wait a while and order a second cup of cappuccino, and ride another taxi back home. That was all I "fancy" like they said in that part of the world. (When you want to let them know that's all you want.)

Singapore is always hot, so we dressed appropriately for hot weather for our trip, it was the end of February, little Jimmy was so cold when we arrived, in Tokyo I had to open a suitcase at the airport to changed his clothes. He was so cold he shivered.

We spent the night in Tokyo, the trip was very tiresome for me, the next day we were picked up by the shuttle and taken to the airport, I heard someone paged "Master James Moore", my son was sitting next to me and I told them so. But they insisted on paging Master James Moore, again, and again, finally, the pager came over ever so apologetic, telling me they could not find my husband, I said, "My husband is not traveling with me. The Master James Moore you are looking for is my son."

We flew to Honolulu, the flight was delayed because there was something wrong with one of the motors, when we finally left, we have been in the air a couple of hours when it was decided to turn the plane back to Honolulu because it was closer than San Francisco, when we landed there, there were fire trucks and Ambulances running along side of the airplane until it came to a stop, then they proceeded to "unload us," I was told to hold my son in front of me to slide down on a plastic chute they had just installed, I open my coat showed the air hostess my belly, I told her "I don't think I can carry another one." "Oh, she said, "I'll take him with me. Jimmy still remembers going down the chute with the air hostess, when they were down, he wanted another ride, I sure didn't, someone went next to me and held my hand so I could go down. We were held there for several hours, I don't even remember how many hours. I got to thinking, this happened to me when I was expecting Jimmy and I promised myself I would never make another long flight again, but I did. And then we flew to San Francisco, and spend another night there. The airline offered to pay for a phone call to notify someone why we were delayed, I said, "no, I'm suppose to stay in San Francisco two days, I'll stay one day, and they won't have to find out. By the time we arrived in Houston, I was talking to myself, I said "Didn't you promise yourself never to do this again?"

I had arranged a hotel tote bag with toys for Jimmy to play with while we were in the plane, so when we were going through customs, he told the agent, "don't you touch my toys." I was so embarrassed, I told Jimmy, "No son, the gentlemen has to look at your toys." But the agent thought it was funny and let him through without opening his toys. That couldn't happen today.

My in-laws met me at the airport, and took me to Kountze, I wanted to get an apartment in Beaumont, Texas, and be close to the hospital. My mother-in-law took me to Beaumont to look for an apartment we wanted a two bedroom, so it wasn't hard to find. I remember I went grocery shopping, before I went in, I asked in their office if it was easy to get a taxi, they told me, yes, you can call from here. So, groceries I bought everything I thought of, so my mama wouldn't have to do without anything and we wouldn't have to go back to the store. I paid for my groceries and asked to order a taxi. No taxi. When one came by it wasn't for me. I was very big and standing wasn't very comfortable, I went back in many times asking for taxi, so finally I said, well, I can't carry the groceries with me, let someone have them since I can't. There was a taxi driver there for someone else, "where are you going?" he asked me, "its only two blocks from here, but I can't take the groceries that far." "We'll take you," they said, they carried the groceries into the house, to my kitchen table and they wouldn't take a tip from me. I blessed them for their kindness.

My mama came from Mexico to be with me when the baby was born, I didn't know if Jimmy was going to be able to come from Singapore for the baby's birth. So I was very happy my mother would be with me this time.

Merle, my brother-in-law, was such a gentle and good man, he took over Jimmy, from the first time we brought him from England, he would hold him in his arms the whole time we were there. Now we were back again, and he took over little Jimmy. He was always full of love for everyone, he was simple a good man.

It wasn't easy to get a doctor because I was seven and a half month pregnant, but I told this particular specialist, if no one takes me, what do you think is going to happen to me? The baby is going to come, anyway." We had Insurance, so that was not the question; Doctors don't want to accept a soon to be mother while she is approaching her eight month of pregnancy. He laughed and took me as a patient, my mother-in-law made the drive from Kountze every day.

Then I received the news that Jimmy would come home on time for the baby's birth. I was so happy because I was scared and I wanted Jimmy with me. The doctor set a date for the baby's birth two weeks before she was due because he didn't wanted me to go into labor. The date was set for May 1st. Labor day. Jimmy just made it home on time.

So the day came, it was a little girl like I wanted. We named her Lois, like her paternal grandmother, I thought she deserve the honor, after all she had given birth to seven sons and the only daughter she gave birth to, had died when she was only two years old.

Lois was born May 1st. 1969. I had a C-Section again because the whole time after Jimmy was born I had problems with the incision, it got infected a number of times and the Doctor was afraid to let me go into labor. He told me, "I'm afraid you're going to burst." "So am I." I answered him. It was funny when I left the hospital; the doctor had already left but came back after he discharged me and said, "Don't go to China too soon." His nurse didn't say anything at the time, but later on, she came back and asked me, "Why doesn't he want you to go to China? It's only about 30 miles from here." I told her, "Because he is talking about Singapore." (There is a small community not far from Beaumont, China, Texas.)

We went to Mexico City only twenty days later. My sister had everything ready to baptize Lois as soon as we arrived, so we had Lois baptized as soon as we arrived. We made a short trip because I didn't feel like traveling so much. It takes longer to get over a C-Section. Traveling didn't help either.

Our trip to Mexico City was very slow, then we travel to Coatzacoalcos to show our baby to the family, only a few days, then we came back to the States.

When we came back from Mexico, Jimmy and his brothers went fishing, they came back very late, after a cup of coffee, Jimmy took a shower and he was shaving, one of his brothers walked to him and told him, "Do you know it's almost two o'clock in the morning? I wouldn't shave at this time for anybody." Jimmy just smiled. But when he left; he kissed me and told me, "Baby, I shave for you anytime."

Then Jimmy had to leave by himself again at the end of June.

Chapter Four

The children and I left for Singapore July 21st, while Neil Armstrong was on the moon, I remembered because they had the speakers so loud in the plane we couldn't hear ourselves speak. Both of the children received their certificate for crossing the International Date Line. It was hard to have to compete to have a bottle of milk warm up by the air hostess, when she had so many alcoholic drinks to serve. When she finally gave me her attention, she brought the milk back at a boiling point. My neighbors told me to report her but I never did, maybe someday, I thought, she will have children and remember me.

I got out off the plane in Hong Kong, only because I was so numb, I needed to stretch my legs, I was exhausted, I sat with my children at the restaurant when I saw this woman sitting with about five or six leashes and a child at the end of each one of them, on her lap, a baby that couldn't have been over two weeks old! When I could close my mouth, I walked to her and offered help. I wasn't as tired as I thought.

Jimmy didn't make it to the airport; he was on Mosalembo Island, Indonesia. But a company man was there, and he took us to a hotel. I had a Suite. After I put the children to bed, I went to bed myself, when a man opened the adjacent door to the next room, and walked in, in his underwear! I screamed and told him to get out of my room. I called the office and asked them what kind of hotel they were running. The manager came, the man that was staying next door came back, apologizing, he thought he was going to the bathroom; he had just arrived himself and thought that door led to the bathroom. I guess it was believable; after all, I was so tired myself I couldn't think.

Jimmy had a house ready for us, no neighbors, it was a commercial area, very busy during the daytime, but at night, everybody was gone. The telephone had not being installed yet. I was trying to get things in order in between looking after the children, and one of the men from the rig brought a servant, a very nice Chinese woman, Aileen. He also brought a gardener. Against the company's advise. I moved in the house.

One day, a man tried to get in, that day Jimmy's friend from the office had shown me where the light switches were, all were by the front door and he helped me locate them. So when the man threatened me with a knife, I told him to leave or I would call the police, he said, "no telephone, no police, he kept trying to poke at me with a knife. I took one of the knives from the cabinets that I was still trying to arrange and told him to go away and leave me alone, he only waved his knife at me, and then I remembered the light switch and turned the outside lights on. It startled him and he ran away. About that time, one of Singapore's famous parades with a dancing dragon leading it, came marching in front of my house, but the house was several feet away from the street, I yelled for help, but no one heard me, the music drowned my voice, the music was very loud, and I realized with the music, I couldn't hear myself scream.

The next day, Aileen came, I told her what had happened the night before, she went out somewhere to make a phone call. People from the office, the police, and a doctor came, because I was in such a state of nerves. I was no good to take care of my children. I was taken to the police station to look at pictures, but when you are shown hundreds of pictures, they all look alike. We never found out who had tried to break in the house, but oddly enough, we never saw the gardener again. The telephone was installed immediately with the help of the police.

When Jimmy made it home, he had already been told about the man going into my room in the hotel, so when he asked me about it, he said, "Do you mean to tell me you had a man in your room and you ran him off?" He always tried to make fun of things to make me laugh.

Jimmy had to take all the passports to the office. In a large envelope, with our Passports, he took little Jimmy with him. When he got to the office and tried to give the passports to the secretary, he realized he had forgotten them in the taxi. He was so worried to take care of little Jimmy he forgot the envelope on the seat. There was no trouble to recuperate their passports, there were American passports, mine on the other hand was a Mexican passport, Mexico didn't have an Embassy or Consulate in Singapore, but it had an Embassy in Djakarta, Indonesia.

In order to reproduce my passport, everyone in the office had to go to the Indonesian Embassy in Singapore, (they had to close the office) and swear that they knew I held a Mexican Passport, until I received a new Passport, I had no papers in Singapore.

Aileen was not only a servant, she was a very good company, but it was hard to communicate, I remembered I was cleaning beans one day, she said. "Missy, Aileen clean beans, how many?" "The whole box" I said. "I put on a pot of water to boil, and told her "when you are finished washing the beans put them in the pot." I went to check on the children, she was right there behind me, I asked her, "How did you finish so fast?" she said. "Aileen fast," I went to check on the beans, she had only washed the hand full of beans I had on the table.

When I told Jimmy about the beans, he said he was trying to get the cook they had on the Mosalembo Island, Indonesia, to cook beans when Jimmy asked him to put one or two small onions, over there, to be clear, if you need twelve of something, you specify by saying one, two, so Jimmy got twelve onions in a pot of beans.

Jimmy came home from work one day, showed me he had gotten a Certificate from Red Adair, he had put out a fire on the rig, and the company had already called Red Adair, so they gave him a certificate, Aileen thought it was a cartoon for a child and threw it out. Later, I found out from one of the other men from the rig that they evacuated everyone from the rig, and only Jimmy and a couple of other men stayed on the rig to put the fire out. Jimmy didn't tell me.

Aileen was washing clothes one day, and when she went to hang them on the line, she ran in and asked me, "Missy, want to see snakes?" I said, "No, where are they?" "Come," she said. I went to the kitchen with her; there was a mama snake and about twelve babies, lying on the slab where Aileen was hanging our clothes. I called the office and asked them what I needed to do. They called someone from the government, they said they like to have control on the kind of snakes there are on the island and how many. I gave notice to out landlord, we were moving out, when Jimmy came home, he said "I signed a lease that we had to give him two months notice." I said. "I'll find a house in two months. We moved to the other side of the island.

Jimmy came from the office one day, I knew there was something wrong with him, and I asked him what the problem was. He said, "Mel Morgan is in town." He said.

I said. "Well?" "Some fellows told me he has been running his mouth that the secretary in Coatzacoalcos was his girlfriend." he came in where we were having some drinks and I let him have it. "He won't say anything about you again." He said rubbing his hand. "Baby," I said, "you know that is not true." "I don't know what he said, but why is that lying so and so is talking about you?"

The next day when Jimmy went to the office, I called Mrs. Murray whose husband just happened to have been assigned to Singapore; he was working for a different company, but Mr. and Mrs. Murray and Jimmy were such good friends. We went out every chance we had. I told her what had happened, I said, "I know where Mr. Morgan is staying, would you come with me? When we arrived, we walked to the reception desk and asked to send a message. Mel Morgan immediately came down and said. "How nice it's to see you again." To which I replied, "I can't say the same. It has come back to me that you have been saying that I was your girlfriend in Coatzacoalcos, and you know that is a lie. He said, "I have never said anything like that." But I knew otherwise. "it's a shame that even when someone always conduct herself with respect and with respect to others there is still someone like you talking; and if I wanted a man, wouldn't you think I would have chosen a better looking and younger man than you?" We left leaving him sitting at the table.

One of Singapore biggest industries it's their great shopping market. One reason, I'm sure, it's because Singapore is a tax free country. And I think jewelry, especially, it's the biggest. In Singapore you don't see newspaper stands in the corners, you find jewelry merchants; their stores are literally full of gold earrings, rings, watches, store after store. And then, there is the thief market, that is the name of the market, I was told the name it's from the time that thieves hid there. When we visited the market, I bought an eight way socket, very necessary in Singapore. We had been invited to a party that evening, when we arrived; they couldn't find a way to plug their blender. I remembered my socket which I promptly pulled out of my purse, all the men thought that was the funniest thing they've seen, they said "I always heard of women carrying everything in their purse, but an electrical socket?"

My next door neighbor's husband was a defense lawyer, he left his law practice for his family's gold and jewelry store where two brothers, and his father managed the store, and it paid him to be a merchant better than to be a defense lawyer.

In Singapore, when you turned in to a street for tailors, that's what you find, tailors, one after another, Jimmy loved silk shirts, and he had them made for him, he could go in the morning and be measured and the next day his shirt would be ready. He also ordered, tailor made pants and suits made here. Jimmy loved those shops.

Jimmy would come from the rig and said, "Let's go to town, baby." And he would take me to a jewelry store he loved, it was the Rolex representatives, he admired the watches, one day, he said, "You know, baby? I'm going to buy me a stainless steel Rolex." I said, No, James, you don't need a watch; you have an Omega Constellation that is almost new. What you want it's a gold Rolex, that's what you're going to get." He was like a kid with a new toy. He wore that watch for many years and he loved every minute of it.

Jimmy came home from the office one day and made me guess who was coming to town. To my surprise and delight I learned The Platters were going to be playing a live show and we were both so happy, we were going to hear our songs in person, they were going to be at the Malaysia Hotel, there was a night club at the top of the building, we sat next to the Sultan of Johore, he had a lot of people at his table, but he was sitting next to Jimmy, and somehow they struck up a conversation about Texas. "Where are your boots?" The Sultan asked Jimmy." Jimmy said. "I don't wear them." "You're from Texas and you don't wear boots?" the Sultan picked up one foot and showed Jimmy his cowboy boots, "I bought them in San Antonio, Texas." The Sultan told Jimmy.

Well, The Platters came out and sang all our favorite songs, we were in heaven. We got to talk to them, asked for our songs and for autographs. I think they were amused at our excitement.

The Sultan invited us to go to his private party after the show. It was in another night club below in the hotel basement, The Platters were there, they sang all night, they sang a different kind of sound. The Sultan invited me to go to Johore, to his Castle without Jimmy after Jimmy left to go to the rig. I laughed it off, but Jimmy didn't think it was funny, even when he was going to back to work several days later, asked me, "don't go to Johore, Baby." And told me, "these men have harems and you will disappear. We'll never hear from you again." I said, "James, don't you know me by now? I'm not going anywhere."

Lois was about eight months old when she started running a high fever, I took her to the doctor; they said it was a reaction to the shot she has been taking. The baby wasn't getting any better, so they decided sometimes they get some of the illness from the shot they were given, she was taking her shots for cholera! We moved into the hospital, they put her in an oxygen tent, they gave her all kind of medications, I never knew what it was, little Jimmy was also was me, we slept where we could, sometimes I found Jimmy sleeping on the floor. The doctor said it was a mild case of cholera, but she was only eight months old. I was very frightened for my baby; I kept thinking about the other Lois, she only lived two years. I was beside myself in fear.

Because the phones didn't always work correctly in Singapore, (at that time), I could receive calls but I couldn't make calls from home, so I sent word to Jimmy about the baby being so sick through a friend, oddly enough it was Mrs. Murray, I found out later she never called the office, so Jimmy came back after Lois was out of the hospital but still very weak,. Jimmy called me from the airport; he was used to me being always at the airport to meet him. So when I answered the phone, he said, "Okay, I lost." "He had made a bet with someone I would be there. I didn't want to tell him about Lois being so sick, because I thought it was best to wait until he got home. Every hour or so, he would call and tell me he was coming home, but then he didn't. When he finally came home, he did so with assistance. It made me so mad that I told his friends who had brought him home to help him into the maid's room, we never had a live in Amah, so no one used that room, and so he could stay there, besides that, it was the only bedroom downstairs.

The next morning, I was packing to come home back to the States and then to go to Mexico with my children. I told him "I'm not in Singapore on vacation, I'm here to be with you, but if after you are gone for one month, you don't have the need to come home, I don't need to be here either." He said. "No, you can't leave me, you know I lived with other women, but not after you, other women have been nothing but a mirage for me, with you it has been real, the real thing, you know you are my life, Blanca, I know I couldn't live with anyone else after you, Blanca, I was born for you." When he said that, I stopped those were the very same words I had told my mother when she wouldn't let me marry him,   I was born for him, and I had said to her the same words all those many years ago. I turned around and looked at him. I said. "All right, but I can't live like this, if you want this family, you have to show me that you want us. I waited for you, our daughter could have died, and you didn't even know, only because you didn't come home."

I never asked him not to have a drink at all, a drink or two was fine with me, but the excess, I didn't accept. I know it was probably because I don't drink myself, I never have. He stopped staying with his friends from the rig, those men somehow lived in bars, some of them didn't have their families in Singapore, and some of the women had gone back to the States. And some of the women were not faithful to their husbands, so they didn't have a solid base for their marriage. Jimmy even stopped smoking; he was ready to do better. He didn't tell me he was quitting and waited until I discovered the ashtrays were all cleaned. He laughed when he was watching me checking the ashtrays and when I realized they were all cleaned, I turned around to see him and I said, "Have you quit?" He laughed.

We met another couple we also made good friends with. Ed and Gloria Kehoe, he used to be in the Blue Angels at one time and now he was flying for an American Airline out of Laos, the families were based in Singapore. They were so much fun to be with, once, they went to Singapore harbor to give the children a boat ride and eat lunch on the boat, the boat didn't have a cabin but they didn't minded, it was a beautiful day, but as usual for Singapore, it started to rain, it became a monsoon, Gloria, like many of us at that time, wore a wig a lot, and she had worn a wig that morning. There was nowhere to hide, and when they arrived at the dock, everybody got out of the boat, and Gloria began to crawl out of it. Her wig had bled the black dye; it was all over her face, she didn't want people to see her. She rode on the floor of the car all the way home. And when they arrived, they all got out opening the door and brought her a towel to cover her face with.

Kamisa, their Amah (Singaporean servant) stepped back when she saw her coming in, she didn't recognized her, Gloria told her, "It's me, help me take this paint off of me." Between Ed and Kamisa scrubbed her to no avail, but they laughed so hard they didn't have the energy to scrub her well. The dye was in the skin and she decided was going to have to wait until it wore out.

Another time, Ed took Gloria to Thailand for the weekend, when they went to eat, she asked the waiter, "What do you recommend?" he told her "Flying fox." She asked "Isn't that a kind of bat?" He said, "No, this is fed only fruit." "Okay, bring me that." She said. When the waiter left, Ed told her, "you know you are going to eat bat. "He said it wasn't bat, I asked him." Ed teased her so much; she didn't believe anything he told her. She was very happy with her dish, and told Ed she was glad she didn't listen to him. When they got home, she went straight to the Encyclopedia to check what a flying fox was, Ed was right, she had eaten a bat. She threw up for two days and then every time she thought about it.

Kamisa's daughter got married but since Ed and Gloria had already left Singapore, I got invited to their traditional Malaysian wedding. I was the only non-Malay woman and the only white man was the groom's boss and his wife. We sat together. The bride and groom attire were made out of the same fabric, and their turbans were almost alike. The food was delicious, all homemade, that was the first time I ate pilaf rice, very different than what you can find at a restaurant. He had been married three other times, not divorced, married, and all the other wives were there with their children, they had something that resemble a throne, each wife had made the throne for the new wife, and when she sat there, the other wives brought their children to her because it's good luck. I took many pictures, there were many rooms and a different throne in each one, I don't know what it means, they told me but that was over thirty years ago. I was very thankful I was invited.

Jimmy riding a rig through Indonesia.

The rig was in Indonesia, they had to wait sometimes for hours for a telephone call, Jimmy said he would come to the radio room with his cup of coffee, everyone else had a cigarette and he didn't and he had to wait there because if the call came and he wasn't there, that just couldn't had happened, he had to send his report to the office , it had to be done daily, and that is how he started smoking again. The nicotine wins every time.

Chapter Five

We came back to the States and went back to Singapore and different places in Australia so many times that it blends in my mind. We went back to Perth; I found a house in the same street as the first house but much further down the road and closer to the river. Jimmy was old enough to go to first grade; Lois went to a school that offered kindergarten instructions for her. And I enrolled in Edwards Business College. I took business and keypunch operator Course, the first computer class of many I have taken since. That course now is called computer programmer, it took one year of intense all day classes. I liked it because Jimmy was gone so much; everywhere we were I would find some school I could go in and learn something.

I could visit my old neighbors, but some of them had left. This house had a park across the street with plenty of games for the children and lots of typical Australian wild trees and flowers. Our next door neighbor had a collie dog and loved our children and protected them. He didn't know Jimmy because he had ridden the rig and when he came home in the middle of the night, the dog wouldn't let Jimmy get close to the door, I had fallen sleep on the couch waiting for him to come home. I had to go outside and talk to the dog for Jimmy to even get close to me. At first, it made Jimmy mad, but I asked him, "Don't you think we are safer with that dog around us?"

I enjoyed going back to school, but it was hard when Jimmy was home and I had to continue going to school or it wouldn't have worked. Once an Australian couple very good friend of ours, invited Jimmy to lunch, there was a Restaurant and Bar in the cellar of the same building as the office. "The Sundowner" His friend was there with his wife, but I was at school, so Jimmy was by himself. Unknown to him, his friend invited some girl at the Bar to eat lunch with them, and ordered lunch for the four of them. When lunch was served, he told Jimmy, "Come on Jim, let's eat." Jimmy saw this girl sitting at the table, and he told them, "No, I can't have lunch without Blanca, when I'm gone to work, I expect her to pay me the same courtesy. Thank you very much." And he left. The same people told me about it and laughed at him. They thought it was funny, I told them "had it been me eating with another man, it would had been different story, would you have thought it was funny then?"

I enrolled Jimmy in a Karate class, he loved it. The first lesson was, they taught him how to scream, I told them he knew that, he needed the rest of the lessons, He was there for one year and he loved it. Once, one of our neighbors who was much older than Jimmy, Jimmy had a board they had giving him to break it with his foot, the neighbor tried to break it with his hand but couldn't do it, Jimmy made a fast turn, yelled and hit the board with his foot and broke it. The neighbor had just turned his head and didn't see Jimmy so he was so surprised Jimmy had broke it, it also embarrassed him, so I told him, "Jimmy broke with his foot." Jimmy told me later on, "Mama, you should have let him think I was stronger than him."

After one year, I graduated from my bookkeeping course and computer class. It wasn't easy but I was proud of my accomplishments, Jimmy was proud I had done it.

Sometimes, we would take the children for a ride by Perth Bridge, in front of it, it was the Swan beer brewery, at night they had a big ship and a sail boat with fluorescent lights. The children loved to go because you could see them at a distance.

Two years had passed; it was time to go back home to the States once again. We came back via Honolulu, we stayed there one week,

Jimmy rented a car and we toured the island. Honolulu is beautiful from the mountains. We flew to Los Angeles, I flew to Mexico City from there, and Jimmy to Houston. A week later, his mother and Earl came with him; my cousin Raul gave us a station wagon with a chauffeur and an interpreter. Earl couldn't believe how modern Mexico is with huge beautiful buildings, exquisite restaurants and modern highways. Everybody had a ball. We took them to the pyramids, museums, just everywhere. We also went to the Plaza Garibaldi; no one could believe the amount of Mariachi groups in it. But it's been a tradition for many years, if you want Mariachis, go to Plaza Garibaldi.

I went to Coatzacoalcos, and Jimmy, his mother and Earl came back to the States. My mother was in Mexico City but the rest of the family on my mother's side was there, I grew up there, so I always wanted to go even if my mother wasn't there. My Aunts were always very proud when I went to see them and my mother wasn't there because they said they knew that trip was for them.

I went back to the States after another week; Jimmy was asked to go to Iran, that was not on his list but he thought, why not? It will be different, so we got everything packed to go to Iran. But because it was a country that not many people could get used to the kind of restrictions they have, it was again required that he should go thirty days ahead of his family.

He left, and then they came for our shipment, it would hopefully be there by the time we got there. Then I got notice from the office. Plans have been changed, we were not going to Iran, the rig had sunk, Jimmy was coming home. In the meantime, Earl was staying with us, he was supposed to go overseas with us, so we got him a passport, we were at my mother-in-law's house, we had been living in Beaumont while Jimmy was there, but since I was leaving too, we moved out.

Jimmy came home, he told me all that had happened, the rig had eleven legs, badly installed, when they were trying to move the rig, four came off, the rig was leaning badly, many of the men were scared and jumped off, they were from several other countries, so language was a problem, they couldn't get through to them that it was safer to stay on the rig than in the middle of the Persian Gulf. No one drowned, but they had to fish a lot of the people out of the water.

Jimmy was very happy that Earl was finally going to stay with him. But Earl changed his mind and didn't want to go overseas. He wanted to stay in the United States.

Jimmy went to Houston's office to talk with them about the Iran rig, when he came back home, he said, well, "Are you ready to go back to Australia?" But first, the company would like for you to take American citizenship because it will make it easier for you to travel. We went to Houston to get some papers at the immigration's office, I had to take an exam and the next month with the swearing in of new citizens I would be changing my citizenship. We went back to Kountze to study for my test.

I passed my test with flying colors; there was American history, "English, Math and any questions they can think of. But I passed them all.

It was very hard for me to give up my citizenship, but it had to be done if I was going to continue traveling. Because of our lifestyle, they took into consideration the time I had been married. Within a couple of weeks, I had my papers and my first American Passport.

We went back to Australia. This time it was Darwin. We went via Singapore and visited lots of friends, then onto Darwin. We were there but our shipment was on its way to Iran. They couldn't stop it, so we were going to have to do with whatever we could until we received our shipment.

We lived in Darwin for four months; we lived in the company house, there was anything we needed there, so while we were there, I started my driving lessons, driving on the wrong side of the road is a different story, although this should be my first driving license. I remember we had company when I got back home from taking my driving test, Jimmy said, "Oh, I see you're driving by yourself." "What did you think that I wouldn't pass?" He said, "I didn't want to say anything in case you didn't passed, I didn't want you to be embarrassed." "Well, you can tell now." I told him.

We bought an old station wagon, not too pretty by big enough for us and our loads of supplies we expected to buy from time to time. It would be handy for camping and fishing trips.

I was toilet training Lois while in Darwin, one day, she ran to the bathroom right after little Jimmy had left, leaving the toilet seat up, when she sat on the toilet, she kind of fell in it, she scream, I ran to check on her, when she saw me she said, "don't flush it mama, don't flush the toilet." When Jimmy got off the rig and I told him, he laughed so hard. When we got home, he picked her up and said to her, "we won't flush the toilet my pretty Baby." Every time he would come near her, he would pick her up again and tell her again, "No, we wouldn't flush my pretty Baby."

Jimmy, another tool pusher and the Company manager were trying to find several tool supplies for the rig, they had to walk from shop to shop looking for it, not very easy in a 100o + heat. So they finally got to this store and asked for their item. Yes, they had it. So they asked the clerk. "How much is it?" The clerk responded "I couldn't give you a clue, mate." They had to go outside to laugh because they didn't want to offend anybody. But it was so hot, their manager said. "It's hot, how about a drink?" "Sure," they both said, Jimmy said they envisioned themselves in one of those air conditioned Bars drinking a cool beer. But instead, he took them to a corner vendor, where they have fruit juices, and offered them a fruit juice while they stood at the corner under the hot sun.

Then we learned of this beautiful community about seventy five miles south of Darwin, the town of Batchelor. At one time it was a uranium mining town. But when they stop mining they started letting other people rent the houses. There were only one hundred houses, at that time.

Several of the families from the company moved to Batchelor. The house we leased was one story house and instead of walls it had sliding glass windows from top to bottom and from side to side of the house to the other, all screened up. We loved it. We could have the whole house open and you would have a breeze all day long.

The dining room had a huge table for twelve people. We bought a small freezer so we could buy enough meat for a month; there were no grocery stores in Batchelor.

There was a lovely family to the back of our house; they had seven well mannered children, there was one about Jimmy's age, Philip, and Glenda were close to Lois's age, so they were both happy they had build-in-friends. Their father's name was Arthur, their mother's name is Beryl, and we became good friends, we still are. Their children are Stephen, Gary, Colin, Wayne, Carolynne, Philip and Glenda.

We have been in Batchelor about two months when our shipment arrived from Iran. It was a huge crate, when it was empty. Jimmy fixed it as a playhouse for Lois and Glenda, and they played there every day, they both loved it.

I learned to eat water buffalo with Beryl, I thought it was good, in fact it was really very good, the children ate what I gave them but Jimmy was another story, he didn't think he would want to try it.

Beryl and I visited a lot, also with her eldest daughter Carolynne, her son Wayne cut grass sometimes. Beryl had a lot of cooking short cuts I learned from her, also, we were far from a doctor and one day, when Lois and Glenda were taking a bath in the outdoor washtub, I turned my head back to watch them; Lois was cover in red spots! She had measles. I got her out of the tub fast; she wasn't running any temperature yet, by that night she was burning up! Beryl showed me what to do. We put her under the shower, then dry her up good and put her under the cover. "Don't cover her head," she told me. Her fever went down. There was no doctor, but a nurse came every week, I believe anyway, Beryl saved the day.

Batchelor had a nice club area, where they played greens or croquet, I gave everything a try, but I am afraid I wasn't very good at it. One day I was walking to the club with the children when we heard a big commotion and people running to the bush, we went to see what it was happening, when we got there, there was an aborigine woman with a big orange and brown snake on her hand! She had run after the snake, jumped over the fence, when she landed on the ground, she had the snake by the head. The snake was dead. I was very happy it was dead.

One of the most colorful men we ever met anywhere was in Batchelor, he was the Park Ranger of that area, Bowen Litchfield, and he told some stories, one was about the time when one of their daughters who live in San Francisco at the time, was there on vacation, and wanted to bring movies of her Daddy wrestling a crocodile, like he used to do when she was growing up, but as his wife said, he didn't remember it had been a long time ago, so he found himself a pretty good size crocodile and proceeded to wrestle with him and the daughter to film it. Mr. Litchfield had a pretty nasty scar from the many stitches he had to endure from that little adventure. They both laughed just thinking about it.

Jimmy fished the whole area, sometimes with people from the rig, and sometimes with Arthur, Beryl's husband. Holly week came around and it was Good Friday when I told Jimmy, if you don't bring a fish today, you are eating a boiled egg for dinner. He came home with a barramundi, it's a big fish, Jimmy found out is the American snook. It was enough for us and all the neighbors, they loved how I cooked the fish rolled in corn meal and deep fried, like is done here in the States.

Lois and Glenda were playing in their "Cobby house" one day, Jimmy overheard Lois tell Glenda, "abracadabra, mate" to her doll. He said to me, "Baby, it's time to go home. And it was time, we came through Honolulu again, we just loved it, we stayed there a week before we got back to Houston."

We came back through Sydney first for a few days to visit with friends and toured the city once again. We were suppose to go to Fiji island but the French airlines failed to let us know we couldn't stay there because there was some kind of strike, so we just flew to Honolulu and stay there another week. Jimmy rented a car and off we went to tour the island.

Chapter Six

Jimmy thought he was through with overseas work, but the company he had been working for didn't have any working rigs in the States. So he started doing research for companies who did have rigs over here. He had to change companies to be able to stay in the United States.

Jimmy found a job in the Gulf of Mexico as a tool pusher, that's what Jimmy liked to do, it was a new company and Jimmy liked the atmosphere there. His new company was Global Marine.

James on a drilling rig.

Since Jimmy was going to be working off-shore, you can live anywhere you want to, we started looking for a house in Beaumont, Texas. Nothing we cared for, and then we looked in Lumberton, and all of the surrounding area. My mother-in-law lived in Kountze, but it's such a small town Jimmy didn't even consider looking for a house there. On the Fourth of July, Merle, came in with the local newspaper, there was a house there we might want to have a look at it.

We went ahead and looked at the house Merle had suggested for us to see. We both liked it at first sight. The owners didn't expect to sell the house so fast; it was the first day that it had been in the paper. We had to wait until they found a place. It didn't take them but another week or so, and we were ready to move in. We went to Beaumont to buy furniture and everything else; we had always lived in furnished houses.

On one of my trips to Beaumont, there were checking for driver licenses, I had my Australian license ready in my hand, when it was my turn, I showed it to the highway patrolman. He laughed when he saw my Australian license, he said. "Ma'am, you need to get yourself a Texas driver license."

The following week, Jimmy and I went to the Courthouse; he was with me because I didn't have a valid driver license. I was about to turn into the Courthouse when Jimmy said. "Baby, if you want them to give you a license, I would get on the other side of the road. You are in Texas now."

It was a lot of fun to shop for our home and arrange everything ourselves. The neighbors didn't know us, but everybody knew my in laws, so everybody came to meet us.

It was July, so Jimmy had plenty of time to get acquainted with other children. Lois was only three and a half years old. We found out of a good kindergarten we could place her in, and we did. Jimmy should have gone to third grade according to Australian school curriculum, but their school year, at the time, ran differently than over here, their school year started in February and ended in November, so he was placed in second grade, because of his age.

Time went by and we fell into a routine with Jimmy working off-shore and when he was home, it was always fishing time. Corky would come on Saturday before five a.m. and they both would drive to the lake.

Jimmy started doing research to build a model drilling rig, he spend hours drawing and measuring everything for a scale rig. He started buying big sheets of brass, then he would come home and cut them for angle corners for the derrick. Day after day. Once, when I visited him in the workshop, as I walked in I kissed him on the back of his neck, he said, "Don't do that." Laughing, later on, he told me he was going to the hardware store, when he came back, for some reason I told him. "Oh, you went all over town with my lip prints on the back of your neck." He was so mad, he said. "I told you not to do that." I thought I would die laughing. I told him. "I never had any lipstick on." I was only teasing you." He came over and kissed me. "I love you." He told me.

He came home from work one day and found all the children in the neighborhood trying to fly a kite, he didn't come in the house, he left his briefcase in the car and took little Jimmy's kite and started running, all the children behind him, the kite rose in the wind. Everyone was happy the kite was flying, that is until two electrical wires snapped. Half of the neighborhood was in the dark for hours.

The next day, he decided he was going to plant a garden with okra, green onions, tomatoes and chiles. He was digging the yard, when one of the neighbors went by with a new digger he had just bought, he stopped, he said, "James, don't dig by hand when you can have a machine. Well, he started using the machine, and fin-ished his garden in no time, that afternoon; the phone company came around to check if our phone was working. They said all the phones on the other street were out of order. The neighbor from across the street came over, Lou Overstreet, "Blanca," she said, we are ready for Jimmy to go back to work." We laughed about that plenty of times.

Jimmy came home from work one day and said, "Baby, we can't keep men working on the rig, they have to go home to catch their wives with somebody else. I want to thank you for giving me peace of mind so I can work, you have given me that." I looked at him, and he repeated, "You have, Baby, you have." I just held his hand; I didn't know what to say.

Jimmy called from the rig one day and asked me to get all his papers ready, they wanted him to go somewhere. When I picked him up in Galveston, he asked me if I had his passport. I asked him. "Where are you going?" He said, "To Panama City." I said," sweetheart, Panama City is in Florida, you don't need a passport to go there." He laughed, he said. "Baby, I'm going to Panama City, Panama."

Jimmy was gone again, he didn't know for how long because he was going to replace someone who had an accident. They wanted him to bring us to Panama, but he thought if we went they wouldn't bring him back to the States any time soon. He was gone for three months.

Before, the most he was gone was one month, three months was a different matter. He came home, and after several nights of love making, after his shower, he sat on the bed and said, "Baby, will it be all right if we just shake hands tonight?" A good sense of humor was one of Jimmy's best qualities.

He continued working off-shore in the Gulf of Mexico, two weeks on and two off. He started building a workshop next to the carport, had a phone installed in his workshop. He roofed the whole thing because the carport didn't have a roof.

I always got along well with my mother-in-law; we went shopping in Beaumont, every time Jimmy was off-shore and of course had long conversations with her. Once she told me people would ask her all her life why she had so many children, she had nine children, the only daughter had died and Don had been a twin (Dan) who had also died, but of my seven living boys, "who would I do without? That it's such a stupid question people ask, I want them all, and that's what I tell them."

Jimmy didn't like to go to Galveston; he was in the Gulf all the time, many times off of Galveston, so to him a trip to Galveston wasn't what he want it. So during summer time, when the children were off from school, we would pack a picnic lunch, and go to Galveston. Sometimes when my mother was here with us, she also loved to go to Galveston and as soon as Jimmy left for work, we made our trip.

Jimmy's model drilling rig started taking shape; we would go to Beaumont to buy whole sheets of brass all the time, and many other tools he needed because everything on the rig was built by him, then he would come home and cut pieces of brass and bend angle iron, lots of them for the derrick he was planning to build. He spent many hours at his workshop, the hours turned into months and finally into years, many years. He would come into the house for coffee and to eat dinner and I would bring him a glass of water because he drank a lot of water. I visited him at the workshop but not for long because he had to do a lot of calculations and couldn't do it talking to me.

I started going to Church in Silsbee, Texas. I met a lady from Guadalajara, who had married a local man, Jesse and Bertha Rodriguez. We became good friends, Jesse and Jimmy liked each other, Bertha and I felt like the family neither of us had here in the States. And no one from our family had come for more than a short visit. When I had surgery and Jimmy couldn't be here, Bertha was the only person who brought me food, when your family doesn't live where you are, that counts for a whole lot. We were good friends for many years.

I had several nice neighbors, but Andrea and her husband Travis Hare visited us, and Andrea and I were coffee friends, we had to have our coffee every evening after work. (At that time I was working at Silsbee Doctors Hospital) Travis and Andrea have two children, Travis Jr. and Danelle. We lived just around the corner from each other in Kountze.

Jimmy had been working constantly in his shop; I kept calling him to come in, it was late. Finally I said, "Do you want me to bring you your pillow over there?" I was asleep by the time he got into bed. The next morning the children and I went to church, Jimmy was back in the workshop already. I was so mad. When we got back, there was a note on the table. "Look in the back yard; I have gone home to Mama. Signed. Me. There was a bird house in the back-yard with miniature shingles, I love birds, he had built me a bird house for my birds. We went to his mama's house; I said, "I came for my baby."

Jimmy came home from South Texas once and brought a big piece of Bois d'Arc. It's a tree, kind of rare or hard to find, it's yellow wood. When he explained to me about it, he said. I like it; it's great to put it on the back of the fire place it will make a good back log. He left it outside, when it got cool, I asked young Jimmy to bring into the house and put it in the fireplace, made a big fire going, I was proud of the fire, and when Jimmy came home I told him he was right that Bois d'arc sure made a good fire. He jumped up and asked me, "Are you burning my Bois d'arc? That was to make handles for different things I wanted to carve." But he didn't tell me! All he said was: "it'll make a good back log for a fire."

Jimmy was due to come home from the rig one day, instead. I received a call from a man who said he was traveling with Jimmy from the rig, and Jimmy had a heart attack on the way to the helicopter. He was in a hospital in Abbeville, Louisiana. I went to my mother-in-law's house to let her know, I'm not in favor to give that kind of news over the phone. I asked her if she could come to the house and stay with the children while I went to see about Jimmy, she said she would call Robert to drive me to Abbeville, Jimmy's truck was in Louisiana, we didn't need another car there. She didn't want me on that road alone, I didn't know where I was going and besides that I was very nervous.

The road was so dark; I couldn't have found the place had I driven there. We got there late, but they let me in to see him, he was in ICU, they told me I could stay on the hall, and there were a few dozen people there already. There was one of the families living in England; Audrey Dugas, her husband had passed away already, I called her to let her know where I was. She came immediately, and invited me to stay at her house, she said "you can't stay here;" I went back in to ask Jimmy. He said. "I feel a lot better if you went with Mrs. Dugas."

A few days later they transferred Jimmy into a private room, I was sitting there with him when lots of nurses rushed into the room yelling "code blue" and then stopped, Jimmy was shaving and some of the monitors he had stocked on his chest had gotten lose. "Mr. Moore," they said, what are you doing shaving?" He said, "I needed it." "Well, you're not supposed to be shaving; I'm supposed to shave you."

That weekend I drove back Jimmy's pick up to Kountze and to check on the children and change cars, we had a Chrysler New Yorker, a lot more easier to ride in than a pick up. The doctor didn't want Jimmy to travel in the pick-up.

Jimmy stayed in the hospital about ten days before he was allowed to leave. I told them who I wanted him to go to and they made him an appointment with a Cardiologist in Beaumont, Texas, Dr. Thomas Lombardo Sr. one of the best in the area. I had heard of him from my days working at Silsbee Doctors Hospital. We had to wait about three weeks before they could see Jimmy.

They wanted Jimmy to have a test, and he had to go into the hospital for that. It was an arteriogram. The doctor came to talk to us; he had to have open heart surgery, a triple by-pass. They wanted him to stay in the hospital that day; Jimmy said. "No, I want to take my son fishing first."

So, we came home and he took Jimmy fishing, they came home late that night, when they got home, I found out while they had the boat in the water, a tree fell in the on the side of the boat and broke young Jimmy's middle finger. Jimmy said. "I didn't want to call you from the hospital because I knew you wouldn't have believed it was Jimmy, you would have assumed it was me.

Two days later, we went to Beaumont and Jimmy had a triple by-pass. He said, but first, I am going to eat what I want, we stopped at a restaurant and he ordered a long hot dog with lots of chili on it, he was hungry for one, and he said, "I know they're not going to feed me for a long time."

It's such a terrible feeling to see the man you love connected to dozens of tubes, and as many needles and he had a tube inside of his mouth. I was there, after the surgery, during the ten minutes visit when he had a seizure, they ushered everybody else out of ICU who were there also visiting, but I stayed, I stepped back, but stayed there, watching his body going into convulsions. It seemed I didn't breathe while the nurses were working on him.

Then they stabilized him, the nurses are really wonderful, collected with such a calm voice talking to their patient, I stayed with Jimmy day and night, only coming back home to visit our children and washed their clothes and take a shower. During the time that we were waiting in ICU, my mother-in-law told me. "Teeny looks good." (Teeny is Jimmy's nickname). I said, "Really?" I thought he looked terrible.

The doctors told me he did great, they said. "He is young enough for this kind of surgery, he is strong and healthy, he will have a good recovery." He was told he had to quit cigarettes, but he couldn't do it, he had me to bring him a cigarette because he said, the feeling was worse if he didn't have a cigarette, so I brought him one. About that time, one of the doctors walked in, gave a good sermon about how he couldn't believe that after what he went through he still wanted to smoke. He was the doctor who operated on his legs, he left and never came back to see him again. (When someone has open heart surgery, they take the veins from the legs to do the bypass for his heart, that's why they worked on his legs.) (For people who are not familiar with this.)

Jimmy couldn't eat hospital food, in fact, he couldn't even smell, it seems like I walked two miles to a Cafeteria to go get him some food, I had bought cans of soup, and heat it up and he would eat that in the middle of the night when he was hungry, but he couldn't stand even to smell the hospital food, I wouldn't uncover the food.

Someone brought the children to visit Jimmy; we had to sneak Lois in because she wasn't old enough to be there. When she got there, she got in the bed with Jimmy, we didn't think anyone would come, but one of the doctors came in, he thought it was funny, as it happened; his mother was my daughter's teacher. He was from Kountze.

We went home after only one week in the hospital, the next day it was Lois's eleventh birthday, I invited Jimmy's family and the neighbors and baked Lois a cake. She was happy with that; I imagine she didn't expect that much with Daddy in the hospital.

The next day, I found a giant 12" hamburger bun at the store. I know it was for something else, it was Hawaiian bread but it was round, so that day, it was a hamburger bun. I brought it home and proceeded to cook a 12" meat patty and all the trimmings for a hamburger, and we sliced it like a pie.

Sometimes, Jimmy wanted to talk about the surgery, it wasn't very often. Once, we had gone to bed when he said. "Baby all I remember is that every time I open my eyes, you were there with me all the time, and I felt I was going to be all right because you were there with me." He would get very melancholic and depressed with teary eyes. Once, he asked me, "What are you still doing here? I'm good for nothing, I'm good for nothing." I told him, "I love you forever James, I'm not here only when you feel well." Then I remember a song we played sometimes, "Don't you know? And it goes, "Don't you know I had fallen in love with you, for the rest of my whole life." I looked for the 8 track tape and when we were in the car, I would play it; he looked at me and smiled. I guess Jimmy and I serenaded each other a lot, but songs can say things we don't know how to say. We also always gave each other little notes, or cards, but mainly just something we write in a piece of paper. Jimmy would trim a heart shape piece of paper, write "I love you" on it and stick it on my steak before he brought it in to the table from the grill.

I called the doctor's office and told him how Jimmy was; I said "Jimmy is not like that, is there a medication he is taking that makes him be depressed?" it was, and he changed it, Jimmy wasn't depressed again.

Then he took pneumonia, his medical doctor told him he should be in the hospital. But I know Blanca will take care of you, so I'm going to let you go home. (He knew me from the time I worked in the hospital), if you do what I tell you to do and take the medications you should be all right. Don't stay in bed too long, that's no good for pneumonia. That wasn't hard for Jimmy to do; he didn't like to stay in bed longer than necessary.

The day that he went for six week checkup, the doctor told him, "you are in top shape; you can do anything you did before the heart attack." Jimmy drove home, then he changed clothes and found him a shovel, went to the backyard, and started to dig a hole, I don't know why, I asked him, I begged him not to do that, he said, "the doctor told me I could do anything I did before." I said, "He didn't know you were going to dig a hole in the back yard."

That night, he was helping me shell purple hull peas, I noticed he was resting his elbows on the table, I looked at his face, and I could see he was in pain. I didn't say anything for a while, and then I asked him, "are you in pain?" he said, "yes," Well, we have to go to the hospital; do you want me to bring a shovel?"

On the way to the hospital, he lit a cigarette, but he already had a cigarette in his other hand. When we got to the hospital, we found out it was only muscle ache. The doctor told him not to abuse himself. I said "it must be an echo in this room."

He was finally feeling better and thought he was ready to go back to work. The doctor told him in no uncertain terms that he wasn't ready yet for his line of work. Because he worked off-shore they had to be sure he could be in a hospital in a moment's notice, if needed.

We decided to go on a trip before Jimmy went crazy. So, we lived in East Texas, so we started a short trip into Louisiana, since his brother, Jack had moved to Mississippi, we drove there, we had friends in the state of Alabama, we went there too. We also went to Arkansas; the children liked it so much they had gone back since. We ended up in Oklahoma, and came down through Dallas. We took the children to the zoo, there was an exhibition there with all kind of knives, Jimmy was very interested it that so he spent most of the day looking at the great election they had.

Jimmy wasn't allowed to go back to work until he was off three months. He was not a happy man staying at home for so long without going to work, he felt great when he worked. Until then, he entertained himself working on his model drilling rig, he spent most of the day in his workshop, and he really enjoyed it. His model rig started getting the shape he wanted, he was happy, that was all about.

Jimmy and Corky went fishing many times, Corky worked during the week, so they had to fish during the weekend, but they always enjoyed each other company.

He finally went back to work; it became a routine again, two weeks on, two off, his brother Corky would come at least once while Jimmy was at home, most of the time twice, and go fishing. Jack didn't fish, and Robert had a different crowd, because he is younger.

**James with his brothers at their mother 80th birthday celebration.
Merle, Robert, Mama, Tyke, Corky, James, Jack, Don (sitting)**

Earl was married by now and living in the Beaumont area, he was working in a work boat that service the drilling rigs in the Gulf of Mexico,, he and Jimmy worked almost opposite to each other, leaving only one day a month to see each other. Earl invited us to go to their house for Christmas, Jimmy was moving a rig at that time besides his tool pushing job on the rig, when he came home to go to dinner to Earl's house, he had been up for two or three days, he would put two chairs together and rest a few minutes to be there when he was needed for the move, then he drove about ten hours, showered and went to Earl's house, with no rest, this was a killer for anyone.

I asked Earl's when we arrived, please don't give your Dad anything to drink because he had not had any rest in days, he is exhausted, and one drop of liquor will knock him out. But, of course, it was Christmas and drinks were served, by the time we sat at the table he couldn't open his eyes.

We stayed for the meal, but then we had to leave immediately, everybody helped him to the car, some guest that Earl had at his house, came to me and said. "Please don't let him drink." I wanted to explode, I told them how he got there, how exhausted he was, we should not have come at all, but then I would have been called some name for not agreeing to come to their Christmas party.

All and all, Jimmy was happy because his family was there, and I was happy for him. My mother came over once a year and stayed a couple of months. Usually, the children and I went to Mexico so I could see my family, then my mother would come back with me.

I love to go to Galveston; Jimmy didn't care for it because he was always in the Gulf. I mentioned to my mother-in-law and she said, "Well, I'll go with you, I like Galveston." My mama happened to be here, so one day we got the children ready, packed a picnic lunch and off we were to Galveston, from then on, we went several times during the summer.

Every summer we would go to Mexico to visit my family, once when we got all together at a restaurant, there was a Mariachi Band playing and I tried to talk above the music to everyone, Reyna Violeta, Rosa Maria, Rosa del Carmen, (Rosi) Amalia, my Aunt Blanca's daughter, Clara Luz besides all our husbands, it was a big table and hard to hear, the next day, I couldn't speak. My son still remembers, how funny everyone thought it was, because I waited for so long to be able to speak Spanish to someone, and the next day after we arrived, I had laryngitis.

I went to my mother-in-law once to ask her if she wanted to go to Beaumont for lunch, I found her raking leaves in her backyard, by the pond, she said, "yeah, let's go." And she dropped the rake on the ground and took off to get ready to go. Sometimes we would meet Adele and Iris who by now, had moved to Beaumont.

Jimmy went to work one morning, soon after that, he called me, they had offered him a Superintendent's position, and asked me what I thought. I said, "I think you should to take it." He said "It means another move, this time, to Houston,"

We put our house in Kountze for sale, and started house hunting in Houston, went to the office first, then looked for a house in the area so Jimmy wouldn't have long drives to work. We found a location we were happy with, where he didn't have to get in the heavy Houston traffic.

Young Jimmy was in High school, Lois in junior high. Both schools were very close to the house. Lois wasn't very happy with her name because some kids called her "Lois Lane," so she gave herself new name, Alexys, from then on, her friends did call her Alexys, we, in the family called her Lois. Her Daddy and I told her, "we can't call you by a different name, you are Lois to us." She understood.

We had our home in Houston built to our specifications; we moved to Houston in January of 1981. Jimmy was always looking for something to do. He found himself building an arbor. The house was "U" shape. In the middle of that "U" he began to build the arbor. I didn't know he could build something like that. I always knew he was very talented, but that arbor was something else. He did most of it by himself; sometimes he had someone to come and help him pick up some of the heavy beams he had to lift overhead. After he was finished, I started with my plants and between the two of us; we had the place looking beautiful. We planted grapes on the sides. He kept saying, "We're just a good team."

In the meantime, Lois kept trying to get her name to be official. It wasn't difficult; I had gotten her a library card under the name "Lexie" they took it as reference, and Alexys was born.

While Jimmy was at Houston office, he was trying to let some Insurance representative know that the OSHA people were going to be on the rig and they didn't allow people with beards on it, Jimmy called them for two days and left them messages with their secretary, but the men did not return Jimmy's phone calls. When they arrived, they found out the OSHA people was there and couldn't do anything about it but shave their beards on the bank plus cold water and they had to do it before they could board the helicopter. They had to shave with whatever they found, someone had a pair of small scissors and they cut their own beards up, they said they had never shaved their beards before, only trimmed them. They were furious at Jimmy, and he told them, "Don't come to me for sympathy; I called you for two days to let you know, and you didn't return my calls. I tried to warn you not to come to the rig. Is not my fault you felt you were too important to return my calls." Anyone who wears a beard would appreciate this story. That's another story is still circulating in the company.

The house in Kountze didn't sell, so we rented the house.

Lois and I were at the grocery store in Houston one day; she wanted me to buy a green mango. When a Hispanic lady told her. Listen to your mother; she knows what a mango looks like when it's green. We got to talking, she was from Cuba, she said, "I have a friend from Mexico," "Really?" I said "I'm from the South," I said, "so is she", "I am from Coatzacoalcos,　Veracruz." I thought that would stop where the conversation was going. But she said, "So is she!" Well, that got my attention, names were exchanged. Her name was Carolina Espinoza del Alba, well, I knew that family very well, she was younger than I and a friend of one of my cousins, Clara Luz, she gave me her phone number. When I called her, and got down about where she lived, it was about half block from my house in Houston. What a coincidence.

We saw each other often, with all the family, or just the two of us; she had her Daddy come to stay with her. It was nice to see her Dad, I also knew him quite well. Her husband Sergio was a very nice man, He and Jimmy liked to visit a lot. Their children are Angelica, Sergio Jr. and Joaquin. Were good visit for Jimmy and Lois.

While we were in Houston, Earl had divorced and was was getting married again. We couldn't attend the wedding because Jimmy was working and the children in school so we were not able to attend.

I had another friend who lived across the street from me, she was from Argentina. They found out Julio Iglesias was coming to

Houston, I still had my Chrysler New Yorker; we piled up in it to the maximum with Julio's fans and went to the concert. We had a lot of fun. Women would scream and Julio smiled and put his finger across his lips and went, Shhh. Because they didn't let him sing.

Then, Carolina and I found out Yul Brynner was coming to Houston with "The King and I" my favorite musical and film. We had to go. Carolina and I were singing a song from the musical, Angelica, Carolina's daughter, an eighteen year old girl, walked away from us. She didn't want anyone to think she was knew us. Carolina and her family went back to Mexico and soon after, Jimmy was transferred to Lafayette, Louisiana.

I enjoyed Houston, so did the children, their favorite groups Def Leppard came to Houston; they had to go to the concert, Jimmy was seventeen years old then and could drive, so they went by themselves, after all these years, they still talk about that concert.

We were in Houston eighteen months, and we had to leave our beautiful home, but fate had different plans for us, Jimmy was transferred to Lafayette, Louisiana.

Chapter Seven

After the usual dozen trips back and forth, trying to sell our house in Houston and trying to buy one in Lafayette, we finally sold the Houston House and bought one in Lafayette.

We all started getting acquainted again with the new people; Jimmy was in his senior year, Alexys was in her freshman year.

Jimmy's sense of humor was always present, once, he was in a big hurry to leave the office for the rig, but he needed to speak with the material's man before he left, the man's secretary told Jimmy she couldn't interrupt him, he was in a very important meeting. So when Jimmy could wait no longer, he clipped an ad from the phone book and slipped it under the door, and left. The ad was from the Bail Bonds. When he came back from the rig, he found out the people who were in the office with the material man, were Auditors, and he was in big trouble. They're still talking about that one at the office.

Everything was fine at school, until Lois was elected in two class rooms as their sweetheart, which qualified her to run for home-coming queen. The local girls didn't accept that, they were fine with Alexys, until that happened.

Then they started harassing her pretty bad, in the bus and at school. I had to go to school every single day. The counselor that she had was against my daughter because he thought she was on drugs, I said, "No, my daughter is not on drugs." He asked me, "How can you be so sure, her eyes are red," I said, "Have you ever seen anyone wearing contact lenses?" He asked me, "Why are you so sure?" I said, "Because I know my daughter, do you know that she invites me to go to the Mall with her? If she was on drugs, do you think she would invite me?" I told him. "Why don't you look at the local girls? They are the problem." Appointments were made with another counselor, when I got there and told him the whole problem, he said, "I can't argue with you Mrs. Moore," and he pulled the middle drawer of his desk, and got out of there the biggest knife I have ever seen in my life. I said, "My daughter was threatened with a knife like that."

Sometimes I didn't send Lois to school because she was so upset, I received a phone call from the school threaten me and Jimmy, we could be put in jail for not sending our daughter to school. I told the caller. "What would you do if they kill my daughter?" I asked for my daughter to be transferred to another school, once again, I had asked before, and no one thought it was necessary. The first counselor told me my daughter had to go to school herself and get her books whenever she left the school. No one else could get the book but her.

By this time, I had taken Lois to a psychologist, he advised me to take her out of that school. I told him, that was what I was trying to do. But we live in that district and that was the school she was supposed to go to. He advised me to ask for an appointment with the school board.

I asked for an appointment with the school board. Jimmy got off from work and went with me. We told them everything. My daughter is running scared. I had to take her to a psychologist, I told the board members, I took a picture of her from the time we were in Houston. I showed them the picture. I said "this is the girl we brought from Houston; A happy, well adjusted teenager. I want her out of that school" I said, "before they kill her." They looked at me, and asked us, which school we wanted her to go to. "But first she has to go to a psychologist." "She has been going, several times." "Okay, we'll make the call now." They said.

She had told me prior of going to see the school board. She wanted to go to Carencro, she had friends who went there, and so we were able to tell them. One of the members of the school board called the school and gave them instructions to give Mrs. Moore, Alexys's books. When we went back to school, they didn't know where to run first, the counselor himself got her books from her locker, carried the books to the car for me, and told me anything else that we needed to just let him know. That was the same man who told me if I wanted my daughter's books she had to come by herself and get them.

There weren't any more problems with my daughter after she moved away and into Carencro School, her grades improved greatly, and finally, she was happy. Of course, I had to drive her to the other side of town, and then pick her up in the evening, but anything was worth my daughter's peace of mind.

We bought Lois a miniature black French poodle, Jimmy and I had asked her what she wanted for her fifteenth birthday, and that's what she wanted. She named her Princess. She still had friends, and one day, when they came over to visit her, the dog started to bark and ran into the living room where Lois and her friends were, and Daddy crawling behind the dog barking, Lois was horrified to find her Daddy crawling after the dog , the boys thought it was funny, everyone but Alexys (Lois.)

Earl called, a baby girl was born, and she was named Leah Nicole.

Jimmy graduated from High School, we all went to the big event, and then we took Jimmy and Lois to a steak dinner.

Jimmy had enrolled in the National Guard in Lafayette; he decided he was going to LSU, so he thought that was the way to go. Since he hadn't decided what he wanted yet, he took classes that generalized in several kinds of majors.

Earl and his wife brought Leah Nicole, and we baby sat with her. We all love to have the baby around. Grandpa built a wagon and pulled her on the sidewalk, she loved it.

In the meantime, there was a rig that was going to Spain; they asked Jimmy if he wanted to go, I had always wanted to go because my grandfather on my mother's side came from La Gran Canaria. But there was a joke around the oil field, "You have to wait until someone dies, to go to Spain." I wanted to go; I knew Lois wanted to go. Jimmy, by now was at LSU, so we went.

Again, Jimmy left. I stayed behind to sell everything we didn't want to keep; besides several cars, and Jimmy's boat and the house, besides lots of furniture. It took about six weeks to sell everything and arrange our trip to Spain. We would make a stop in England, Lois wanted to go to Sheffield, and since we were going that far. I thought we have a visit with Thelma and Elspeth.

We went to New Orleans to get our Passports, stayed a couple of days in a motel while we finished things in the states, and then Lois and I left for Kountze. When we arrived, the big news was that there was an airplane hijacked in Greece, they wanted the heads of every American on a platter. It was 1984. That was the beginning of a problem that lasted for many years. Well, whatever happened, I was going to meet Jimmy in Spain.

We had our dog Princess with us, but because we were stopping in England for several days, we had booked to go to Spain direct flight, so she wouldn't have to be put in quarantine in England. Even now, is still a lot of fun to talk to my daughter about our trip together to England, as soon as we arrived, we went to our hotel and took a train from Victoria Station to the city. London is a beautiful city, and Lois couldn't get enough of it, we got in one of those buses for tourist which we certainly were, and toured away. The next day, we took the train to Sheffield; I hired a taxi for several hours, and Lois had the luxury of telling the driver where she wanted to go, and she wanted to go everywhere that had anything to do with Def Leppard. The taxi driver asked me, "aren't you concern because your daughter it's such a fan?" I said, "She is not hurting anyone, is she? This is what she likes to do; I don't see the harm of it." To which he agreed. Lois told me she will never forget her trip to Sheffield. After the grief she suffered in Lafayette, she deserved to have something pleasant in her heart.

We took a train to Scarborough, the scenery was beautiful, Lois took pictures and dated them, June 17, one day we were looking at pictures, and years later, we checked the date that was the day she got married. Then we went to Scarborough, and Keith and Elspeth were there to meet us. We were the last train. We went to Filey. It was so good to see Keith and Elspeth again. They were just as pleasant as before. This time their eldest daughter Rachel was working in Ireland so we didn't get to see her, but they had their youngest daughter Emma with them, just as pretty as the rest of the family.

Elspeth took us around to see everything. Of course, it has been so many years everything looked different. Then we went to visit Thelma, we had some pictures taken of the three of us. They had met while we were there but were not that friendly, well, after we left England they saw each other more and they became good friends. We had lunch at Thelma's house, one of the twins came over with her baby, there were both married but only one of the twins could come by.

We went back to Elspeth's house and had dinner there, I invited them to come to Spain, but their summer vacation plans had already been arranged the year before, which is a British custom. After a good visit we went to bed, the next day they took us to the train station. It was a good visit.

From there we went to York, I knew Lois would like it, only the walls around the city are good enough reason for anyone to make the trip. We stopped there for a few hours, and then continued our trip to London.

We flew to Spain, everyone applauded when they announced we were about to land in Barcelona and the sun blinded us, like a sign of our next stop. Jimmy was there waiting for us. It was as usual, such a happy reunion. He took us by the highway that runs next to the Mediterranean Sea, what a trip! And what a road! The road winds up, and it's like following a blind mule, those were Jimmy's words, not mine.

The office was in San Carlos de la Rapita. Jimmy had found a beautiful apartment overlooking the Mediterranean Sea, every time I would sit on our front terrazzo, I didn't want to get up. I just didn't need to go anywhere else, I was there. Princess as happy to see us, and we were happy to see her. Jimmy said he would have been happier if we wouldn't have sent her with so many ribbons. He said, you wouldn't believe the looks I got at the airport when I had to cross it with a dog with pink ribbons.

We had to find a school for Lois to go to, there was one in Barcelona, but it was a Boarding school, Lois had enough grief in Lafayette, Jimmy and I decided to find a different answer for her school issue. We found a French teacher in town, and so for now for her to speak another language would be enough for now; she also did pretty well with her Spanish and Catalan. Not too many people can speak four languages.

On the ground floor of the apartment building we lived in, there was an office where they sold boat part of every kind anyone would want. The girl in there was Anna Viscarro; she worked for her Dad, she and Alexys became best friends, from the first day they met. And I became a pretty good with her mother, Esperanza. Anna and Alexys (she didn't used the name Lois in San Carlos)they went together everywhere, I met her mother, and so, because I am from Mexico, our customs were very similar, I knew they danced until late, they laughed at everything and were very happy people, like I remembered when I was home. It reminded me of being at home in Mexico, I felt good being there.

We all had many friends, there was a barbeque every weekend at this beautiful Villa, people from the office invited us, after that, we became good friends. There was a large swimming pool in it and the kids enjoyed it tremendously, Lois couldn't have been happier, she was learning to speak Catalan, and everyone spoke Spanish to me, but Lois learnt Catalan, it seems that because I am from Mexico, they accepted that I don't speak Catalan, from anyone else from outside Cataluña but inside of Spain, they don't want to speak Spanish to them, that is what I was told. They said, let them learn Catalan.

There was the Mercado or market every Saturday and everyone went, if you wanted to see someone, that person would be there Saturday morning, and it was a lot of fun, bought a lot of things we didn't need, I guess it is a lot like the American flea market. Lois's friends would come to the house to drink a cup of coffee with plenty of milk, like we drink it in Mexico. I found out we had more in common than I ever thought.

We went for walks by the water; I couldn't imagine what a difference the water can make, especially when it is the Mediterranean Sea. One thing about that region is that the tap water was salty, and I mean you couldn't brush your teeth in it; we would make a weekly trip to a place where there was a water fountain with sweet water. Or you could buy water in the stores. But don't drink the tap water.

In Spain, every little town has their own week for their time to organize their Fiesta. In San Carlos, their Fiesta was in July, and boy!, they celebrate. Since we lived by the water, they set up the fair with complete loud speakers and all the music anyone wants to hear. All night long, until about at least four o'clock in the morning, Jimmy was moving rigs, and he had just come back from Greece, we had just dropped to sleep, when people started singing, they have a route they go picking up people everyone on the way, they walk across the street arm in arm, singing, I thought it was beautiful, but Jimmy was very tired, he had not had hardly any sleep. He picked up his head and said, "Do these people ever sleep?" We all laughed when I told them. The first day was the running of the bulls, and San Carlos didn't have nearly as many bulls as Pamplona, but enough for us.

In Spain, it seems like every day is a Fiesta of some kind. One day I was going to do some shopping, there were lots of people in the park celebrating, several girls dancing "la jota aragoneza," it brought back memories from home. I danced that while in school.

We would go to Barcelona shopping and for lunch, we could take a bus in town, and ride it to Barcelona. It would leave us at El Corte Ingles, one of the best stores in Barcelona, whether we wanted to buy something or not, we would have lunch and have a great time. Also, I was invited to join a group in San Carlos, "Las Amas de Casa" or the housewives Club. We were about thirty women, and we met every week, that was a lot of fun.

Before we were there for six months, we had to get out of the country to have our passports re-stamped, so Lois went to London with a friend of ours from Chile, her name is Irma, she has been living in San Carlos for many years. Jimmy and I went to Andorra, a small country between Spain and France Jimmy drove the company car, we were told it would take us about four hours to get there, we made it in nine because Jimmy drove into every little road that looked pretty and everything looked so beautiful he didn't want to miss anything.

We also befriend another couple from Chile, Eliana Vasquez and Pedro Vargas, we always had a lot of fun with them, Pedro was a very happy person and fun to be with. They had two sons, Yuri and the baby.

Young Jimmy went to Spain for Christmas, but Daddy just couldn't make it home, he was in Cairo, he came home to Barcelona via Rome, just before he arrive in Rome, there was a big shooting at the Rome airport. Many people were killed. It was Christmas 1984. We went to the airport in Barcelona to pick Jimmy up. The people were up in arms and the soldiers at the airport were all armed. I have never seen that anywhere we have ever been, but the problem was very serious and all the airports were the same. Jimmy said every airport he was at, was the same.

James and Blanca, young Jimmy, Alexys and Princess in Spain

Jimmy got a few days off to take our son to visit the ruins, like Morella, which is a beautiful place. It used to be a castle. All it was left was the walls, it's on the hills and it was a large castle. We went to Peñiscola, where "El Cid" was film, we lived close to it. It was south of San Carlos. I loved it. It's a very small island, you can drive up to a certain level and then you can walk the rest of the way. They have coffee shops on the way and you can have something to drink if you need to sit down. The beach there was a topless beach. We didn't notice until after we had ordered our meal, I was very relaxed sipping on a drink when I saw this woman walking with only her bikini bottom. I know my eyes got bigger when I looked at Jimmy's way, both Jimmy's were just waiting on me to find out where we were. I acted very sophisticated; I didn't panic. I took a sip from my drink and asked where my food was. They busted laughing because they have been watching me all along for my reaction, when I finally saw the topless bathers.

Jimmy came home from Cairo; He didn't feel like celebrating Christmas he was so tired, but we celebrated anyway. At the very least, we were together. We celebrated our holidays whenever Jimmy was home. This wasn't any different. Jimmy got a few days off, but first, he had a phone call, they needed him back in Cairo; I motioned to him, to let me make his reservations. He told them, and I made reservations for him from Barcelona to Cairo, there was no need to go to Rome. So he went to Cairo, he had plenty of time to go to the pyramids; he rode a horse, the company man who went with Jimmy, wanted a camel, they rode around the pyramids, then the company man couldn't ride the camel and asked Jimmy for his horse, Jimmy told him, "we both got what we asked for."

He brought me and Lois jewelry from Cairo, very pretty and different. We took Jimmy shopping, and then it was time for him to come back to the States, It was hard, but you do what you have to do.

I started trying to look for my Grandfather's family, my mother's father, he was from Spain. Sometimes when people immigrate to another country they lose contact because in the first place he was a young man when he left La Gran Canaria, one of the Canary Islands, but he went to Mexico by himself and died when my mother was a child. So there was no way to find out anything about his family. I knew from the beginning it wasn't going to be a successful venture.

Lois was very happy there, it saved her life when we moved to Spain, and she told me that it was like a medicine to her.

Jimmy was being sent all over the Mediterranean moving rigs, so much that I was asked if he worked for the CIA! His rig didn't get the contract they expected to be renewed. But Jimmy was sent to move rigs. So he was busier than ever. He went to Greece, Italy and Egypt several times to move rigs. Once when he went to Egypt, after he arrived in Cairo, the rig was on the other side of Cairo and he was driven through the desert a long distance, in the middle of the desert there was check station where they checked every ones papers, he said he couldn't believe it, there was nothing anywhere but that little station.

Then our year was over and it was the end of end of Jimmy's contract, we had to come back to the States. Lois didn't want to come back, she and all of her friends cried their little eyes out but I told them, we can't leave Lois here, she had just turned sixteen years old. Even the experience in Lafayette wasn't as hard as having to leave Spain for Lois. It was hard for me as well. I received several gone away parties. And that's how life is, you do what you have to do.

Because Jimmy's rig was not working, it had to be stacked, Jimmy had to retire. He was one of the lucky ones; some of the other men were not old enough to retire and they just had to be let go, because there were not enough working rigs.

Valencia was south of San Carlos and I enjoyed going there, just looking everywhere and stopping at a restaurant was sufficient for me. And I loved their paella. We went all the time whenever Jimmy was home, everything was new to us, so even fishing, we used to go to the Dam by the Ebro river, there was a hotel there he went when Jimmy wanted to fish. An American base or some American company stocked the dam with bass and trout. Jimmy loved it; he fished alone because there was no one fishing but him.

Earl called, it was March and he was a proud father of a bouncing baby boy. His name was Matthew.

Before we left Spain, Jimmy rented a car; the company car had to be turned in. Lois stayed at Ana's house; she didn't care about going anywhere or seeing anything, only wanted to stay with Ana. Jimmy and I toured Spain. We drove to the south to Murcia, he turned left, and went all the way to Andalucía, to the night clubs to watch them dance Flamenco, they were incredible flamenco dancers, and when you think you saw the best dancer, a better one would come out.

While we were there, I notice a group of young men kept watching Jimmy and talking to each other, then they started walking towards us. I told Jimmy, "Don't speak English, let me talk." Then I started to tell him about the trip in Spanish and leaving our daughter and the dog back in San Carlos." Then I smiled at them and said "Hi." To them, they bowed their head to me, as to return my greetings; it looked to me like they're going to start a problem with Jimmy. Then they turned around and left.

We also went to Granada where the Alhambra is, the beautiful hand work of the times when the Moros were in Spain, went back to Toledo, drove outside Madrid because we have been several times, toured all the way back to San Carlos de la Rapita. Went by a place where they have several huge wind mills, we were told that the place where Sophia Loren made "The man from la Mancha" We went by another place where there was a Church we couldn't go in because they closed in the middle of the day; we read the plaque where it said there was a statue presented to them from Veracruz. I wanted to wait, but time was important to us, we had been driving everywhere and Lois has been all this time at Anna's house. And we couldn't wait. Several castles on our way that was always something I enjoyed.

The night before we left San Carlos, all the girls were with Lois, they stayed as late as they were allowed to stay and then it was time to leave. We had to bring Lois almost by force.

Chapter eight

We came back via Amsterdam. When we arrived in Kountze, we found Mama very sick; she stayed in bed most of the time. She had lost a lot of weight and she was too weak to leave her bed.

It was good to retire but with Jimmy at LSU, and Lois, we needed to keep working, Lois decided to go to Lamar University and present the equivalent test for High School. And that was a good decision because you can go to any college and graduate of whatever you want to. Lois has taken many computer courses, and she is very good at what she does. Her Spanish is excellent even if she doesn't have the opportunity to practice her Catalan. But Ana and Lois still called each other occasionally, and they speak Catalan.

Jimmy and I made a decision, we would open some kind of business, we didn't know what yet, we had to make some research and find out what we wanted to do.

First of all, Jimmy wanted to live in Jasper, Texas. He said, he always wanted to live in this area because of the fishing, the Angelina River runs North of Jasper, and there are three lakes, Dam B, Sam Rayburn and Toledo Bend. We own a beautiful home in Kountze, a brick home, so it was out about bringing it over here. We started by trying to get us a place in Jasper and go from there. Young Jimmy came back from LSU and said he didn't want to go back there. But when he said it, it was too late to be enrolled anywhere else.

When we came back from Spain we stayed at my mother-in-law's house, I cooked, washed clothes, and then I got very sick, I had very high fever, my mother-in-law told me, she thought I had rocky mountain fever, because Adele had removed a tick from my back. But the doctor dismissed that and said I had brought the flu from Spain, I said "I don't feel I have the flu," he replied, "who is the doctor here, you or I?" He gave me antibiotics for the flu; my fever would stop for a while and then would come back again. We went to Beaumont and bought a beautiful Blazer Chevrolet, we both love it.

In the meantime, unexpectedly, Adele died, she was a bad diabetic and she didn't take care of herself, anyway, Jimmy went to Corky's house to spend the night with him. We were still trying to organize our plans to put up a business together.

We found a place in Jasper and bought it, Jimmy was busy visiting his mother and helping me with our arrangements with the store. We had decided it would be a ladies' clothing store, so we went to Atlanta and brought back a Fashion Designer to help us, we wanted the store too look professional, and between them and the courses we took in Dallas, our window dressing in Jasper were very pretty.

We named our store Exclusive Fashions, and worked vigorously all the time, to accomplish what we wanted. We shopped at Dallas market, we would order some fashions from Atlanta because they had a program where they send catalogues with the Fashions, which it was very good for a small business. We had the store open for almost ten years.

The school started everywhere and Jimmy couldn't get in for that semester, he thought he would want to go for a Defense Lawyer, but it would be a while before he could get in. I told him, you have to look for something to do, you can't be here doing, nothing. So he got ready and went to Beaumont, when he came back, he had signed up in the Navy. But again, he couldn't leave until August and it was early in the summer. I said to him, get you a little job somewhere, but stay busy.

Jimmy went into the Navy, and after his training, he applied to get in a Nuclear Submarine, they had the FBI investigating him, In

Kountze and Jasper, they couldn't even have a traffic ticket which he didn't have, and he was accepted.

My fever came back; I was so bad I was almost too weak to walk, when the Doctor saw me and after I told him what had happened, he ordered a blood test, which the other doctor never ordered, he gave me one antibiotic, he said if I'm right, you can get the rest of the antibiotics tomorrow, when the blood test came back, I had rocky mountain fever. He said. "Mrs. Moore, people die from this and you have been walking around with it for four months."

My mother-in-law started getting worse, Jimmy would go to Kountze every day, in only a couple of months after we open the store my mother-in-law passed away. I closed the store a couple of days to be able to go to the Funeral.

Corky started coming every Tuesday, then he and Jimmy would go fishing on a Wednesday, I guess they console each other with their loss. We missed Corky if he didn't come, when Jimmy asked him what had happened. He said "I don't want to impose on you with my presence." I told him he was always welcome, I said, "I thought it was enough Teeny had told you to come over any time, but if you need re-assurance, you have it from me, you are welcome to come any time. I said, "We prefer you call only because we don't want you to have to wait outside." He laughed. And from then on, he came every Tuesday afternoon and go fishing every Wednesday, sometimes I would cook at home, sometimes we would go out to eat dinner. I remember we went out and Corky took his jacket off at the restaurant and hung it on the back of his chair, when we left the table corky forgot his jacket, Jimmy stopped and put on Corky's jacket, while we waited in line to pay the bill, they have talked ten minutes before Corky noticed Teeny was wearing his jacket.

Lois met a young fellow still in High school, Kelvin Flowers, when I enrolled Lois in a Fashion school she had decided wanted to attend, then he asked her not to go to Houston because he was still in school, so she said she had changed her mind, instead, as soon as he finish high school, they were getting married, with all the trimmings, her friend from Spain, Ana Viscarro from San Carlos, also came for the wedding, she was the Matron of Honor, she also had seven bride maids and seven grooms men. My mother came over from Mexico for the wedding. The reception was at the Church Hall and then there was a dance at the Lions Club. The next day, they left for Galveston to go to their Honeymoon.

I always remember Jimmy's sense of humor, once, Kelvin's mother Eunice, came over, I knew she liked to drink coffee, so when I saw her driving up our driveway, I got up and put on a pot of coffee, I asked Jimmy, do you want another cup? He said, "No, I'm still drinking this one," Young Jimmy was here at the time, he wanted a cup, so I put on a full pot of coffee. We started talking when Mrs. Flowers came in, when coffee was ready I started to serve, but I didn't pour Jimmy any coffee before he had told me he didn't want any. When I put the pot back on the burner, he got up talking to himself, "Moore, do you want a cup? Yes, I believe I do." He answered himself. I said, "I thought you said, you didn't want any coffee." He said. "Didn't you know I would change my mind?"

My mother was with us when we celebrated our 30th wedding Anniversary; we didn't celebrate the 25th because young Jimmy was still gone in the submarine, but he was back for our 30th, and working in the area. So we had our Vows renewed. It was beautiful; Father Ron had us stand at the Altar to recite our vows. It was simple, but to us. It was moving. We had a small reception at the Church Hall.

James and Blanca, Earl, Alexys and James junior.

Then Jimmy started having heart problems again, I saw him taking nitro tablets, he couldn't deny he had been having trouble but didn't want to tell me. I made an appointment with the Cardiologist the next day; he was admitted to the hospital immediately. The cardiologist came out to talk to me, the problem was pretty bad; he told me Jimmy had had a heart attack and this time his heart had been damaged. It was working with only part of the strength, we had to be very careful, no smoking. His nurse spoke to me later on, the first thing you need to know is: don't nag him about smoking, he is a big boy and he knows smoking it's bad for him."

He had a slow recovery, Corky and Jack came over to drink coffee with him. I remember once, Jack, Corky, Robert and Father Ron were all here in the kitchen drinking coffee with Jimmy. Corky would come every week and take Jimmy fishing, he would tell me, "Blanca, don't worry about Teeny, I'll take care of him. He loves to fish, and if that is his time, he rather goes in the middle of the lake while fishing." I agreed with him. Robert and Iris would visit Jimmy at times.

Kelvin joined the Army, and while they were over there, Lauren was born, August 6th 1990. She was born in Augusta, Ga. Then after a couple of years Kelvin had an honorable discharge from the Army and they came back to Texas. They went to the Houston area, because of the job situation being better over there.

Merle was sick but would send gifts to Lauren all the time, when they got back, Kelvin and Lois would go to Kountze every chance they had to visit Merle. He loved Lauren, and Lauren felt Uncle Merle needed her love because she loved him back and he just "ate that up."

James with the rig he built

Then Merle health deteriorated very much, Jimmy would go over to Kountze as often as he could, he wouldn't let anyone take him to the doctor, once, he asked Jimmy he was ready to be taken to the Veterans Hospital in Houston. We all knew what that meant. Merle lasted two weeks; we were there when he fell in to a coma. And Jimmy was asked to give permission to disconnect Merle from the machine. He told them he couldn't do it by himself, there were other brothers involved, so he called and everyone agreed Merle couldn't come back again. And to give the approval for his brother to be disconnected was very hard on Jimmy. Merle was brought to Kountze for his Funeral.

Later on, Don was diagnosed with Alzheimer's disease and admitted at a Nursing home.

The business wasn't doing well; we have been at that location for seven to eight years and we moved to another location downtown Jasper, and only one year in that location, we decide to close the store for good. But I felt the need to work outside my home.

For about three years after Jimmy's heart attack. Corky came religiously every Tuesday, have dinner with us and he and Jimmy go fishing on Wednesday morning. But this week, he didn't show up, and Jimmy started calling Corky, time and again and Corky didn't answer. We were alternating the calls and when I called one of those times. Someone answered the phone, I didn't recognize the voice, I said "who is this? What are you doing in my brother-in-law's house?" he said "Ma'am, I am the Police, your brother-in-law has been found dead on the kitchen floor, it seems he passed away last night." He was at home by himself, we had been calling him for two days and he didn't answer, other people had called as well, but he had left the garage door open and he didn't do that, so the neighbors called the police, and they found Corky on the floor, he hit the floor hard, his skull was cracked there was blood every-where. I called Lois, to go over there because she was the closest one to Corky's house of all of us. When they arrived, the Police was still there, Kelvin cleaned Corky's blood off of the floor so Jimmy wouldn't see it. He suffered enough with his brother's death. They estimated he died the night before, while he was fixing himself a roast beef sandwich, everything was on a board ready to be fixed and he was on the floor, they said he never knew. Understandable, Jimmy took his brother's death very hard, He kept saying, "No, it's too soon, it's too soon."

In the meantime, my cousin Clara Luz also died suddenly of a brain aneurism. She was 50 years old.

Jimmy was a war veteran from the Navy; he went to China, right after the war. We had been to a Reunion years back when they held the Reunion in Baton Rouge, this time when we received the Newsletter; they announced the Reunion on a Cruise to the Baha-mas, when I read the Newsletter, I told Jimmy, "Sweetheart, We are going," he smiled, I had been wanting to go on a cruise for years, but with his line of work off shore all the time, he never considered it. He would tell me, "I'm at sea all the time; I'm not going back to sea again." We never went. But now, he couldn't say that. He said. "All right, let's go, make all the arrangements and we'll go." He didn't have to tell me twice. We flew to Miami, we stayed there overnight, seven days cruise and two extra days in Miami on the way back. It was a beautiful trip.

I was working at this time for East Texas Support Services, and had my vacation time for this trip.

Prior to them, I worked for about three to four years at Hart Industries, as a Representative for Mr. Dewey Hart, made monthly trips to Mexico to Telefonos de Mexico to sell creosoted telephone poles for the Mexican telephone company. When he closed his company, I went to work for East Texas Support Services, I worked for the Transportation Dept. first, and then I went to work as a case worker, the reason I always wanted to work is because we kept a maid and a nurse for my mother and my aunts, and it was expensive, I wanted to help out with the finances, I worked until I retired five years later, my mother and my aunts had all died by then.

A couple of years went by and Tyke, the youngest of the brothers passed away, he was found dead in the morning at his home in San Antonio by his brother Robert. He had phlebitis, complications from it killed him. They had visited the night before, and on his way home,and out of San Antonio, Robert went to check on Tyke before he left, and found him dead.

Jimmy and I decided to go to Mexico for Christmas; I don't how many years it had been since I had been home for Christmas, we always went during the year, but we were too far to go home for Christmas, after we settle in the United States, Jimmy was always due to come home from work the day after Christmas and I didn't want him to come to an empty house, so I wouldn't go home. In all of my married life, I only went home twice, maybe three times. That I remember. We had a grand time, all the family was there and we went to all kind of parties.

We have Posadas, the nine days that Joseph and Mary looked for a place to stay before Jesus was born. At this particular "Posada" the entertainers were between 25 to30 men playing guitars, and when they walked out playing, they caught me by surprise and before I knew, I was crying, no one knew why, but I did, I haven't seen anything like that in so many years, I was sobbing and I couldn't stop myself although I was trying hard. And they played old songs I have forgotten. I saw people dancing in such a happy way; I had forgotten people get that happy just dancing, I saw the happiness in their faces.

The next day, Rosi and Ramon invited us to their home for lunch, which it's our main meal, they had also invited Ramon's boss, he was late, and so, he had called them with an excuse for being late, When he finally arrived, he came with a group of guitarist; he said he was late because he was trying to find a "jarana" a group of players of typical music of the state of Veracruz, their main instrument it's a harp, plus different kinds of guitars. He had seen me at the party the night before and was overwhelmed when he heard I had not being home for Christmas in so many years. The musicians stayed and played for several hours.

Then my Aunt Lucha died, we believed she was 105 years old. A year later my mother died, she was 95 years old, but there was no time for me to go because they called me the day she was buried, since I am from the South, I have to change planes in Mexico City. A year later, my Aunt Quina passed away. So the old generation was gone.

While at work for East Texas Support Services, I became very sick, no one could find out what was wrong with me, my doctor in Jasper told me, "Mrs. Moore, I don't know what to do with you." So, one of the women from work told me to go see her doctor in Beaumont. She made the appointment for the next day. He decided to put me in the hospital for tests. And they thought I needed an arteriogram, my arteries were clogged 90% and 95%. The cardiologist told me right there in the operation room (because you are aware of what it's going on at all times), I was a heart attack waiting to happen. What do your advice?" I asked him. He said, I need to place a stent in those arteries." When do you think you'll do the surgery?" "Right now." He said. "I didn't know this is done as part of the arteriogram." And he place two stents that day.

A couple of days later, I had a huge bruise in my leg. I called then and asked them why that was there. They asked me to go to their office the next day. It was an aneurism. They said. "We might be able to seal it, if we can't we'll have to go in." So they worked on my leg trying to seal the aneurism, it's very painful, but I was very relieved it sealed.

But I couldn't get better, I couldn't walk, and my energy level was very low, The Beaumont medical doctor sent back to work, He told me there was nothing wrong with me, I told him "the way I feel, they wouldn't let me in the door, and I wouldn't blame them." I saw his face when Jimmy was helping me up from his office table; he looked at me and shook his head. He thought I was putting   on an act!

I went back to the Cardiologist and told Sheila DeVaugh, P.A., what had happened, and I said to her, "I can't go back to work like this." She said. "Absolutely not, I'm going to give you a doctor's excuse so you don't have to go back to work until you are ready. And she ordered a chest X-Ray.

The X-Ray showed I had a large gall stone, everybody who talked to me said they never had seen a bigger stone than mine, I might add, what two M. Ds. couldn't do with me, a P.A. did, I would go to Sheila DeVaugh any time. They didn't let me ride with Jimmy, I had to ride the Ambulance to St. Elizabeth hospital in Beaumont, Everyone in the hospital tried to get my vein, but they said because I was so dehydrated no one was able to, and then just before they took me to Beaumont, someone did, so they could place an I.V. for the trip.

When I arrived in Beaumont, my daughter Lois was there waiting for the Ambulance, that was a big relieve for me, when we went in, they couldn't attach any medications to that needle, so they had to pull that needle out and they started again to put another needle, they had poke both arms in different places and both feet, I got to where I wasn't feeling what they were doing to me, it seems at the time, I didn't care. I was told they had sent for the medic from the helicopter, but I was taken to surgery before he arrived and before I was taken in, they open a place on my shoulder to get a vein. I was out after that.

I asked the surgeon to let me see the stone, he said. "I have never seen a bigger one, but your stone it was broken in a million pieces to take it out of your body, so I'm sorry, but it can be put back together again."

They had called, my medical doctor who said it wasn't anything wrong with me and to go back to work. When I saw him coming into my room, I couldn't believe it, but the cardiologist admitted me to the hospital, so they had to have an M.D. wanted to ask him so bad, if he thought I was sick enough to be in the hospital, but I said nothing. Only, I made sure the Cardiologist's office knew he wasn't my doctor any longer.

Jimmy brought me home after five days in the hospital, but when six weeks check up was due, he couldn't go with me, he asked me if I thought I could made the trip alone. Its 75 mile to Beaumont from Jasper, but when he asked me that, I knew he wasn't feeling well and I asked him, he said. "No, I just don't feel up for a trip like that." I had needed a lot of help while I had been sick and his energy level was nil. I remember once we went to the grocery store, when we got back, we're both trying to carry as many bags as we could so the other wouldn't have to carry anymore. It was before my six weeks check up, I had several bags in each hand, and when I got to the porch, I couldn't get on it. Jimmy looked at me and said, "Baby."

I could have gone back to work, but I though, at my age that was enough work, so I retired. My mother was no longer here, so I didn't have to send her money. Jimmy was very happy I was going to stay at home, and so was I. After I was strong enough we made several short trips in the surrounding area for recreational vacation.

The following year, Jack was very sick with cancer, we went over to see visit him, it was the 17th of December, Jimmy said he had a good visit with Jack, he was happy and laughed out loud, Elmarie told me he hadn't laugh like that in a long time. Her eyes were filled with tears. Jimmy was happy we had visited Jack before he died. Jack died two weeks later, December 30th.

Years went by; Jimmy and I have been married 41 years. It was February, the weather was miserable. When he had something like bronchitis, against his better judgment, he let me make him an appointment, the doctor ordered and X-Ray. Because he saw something in one of his lungs, he sent him to Beaumont to a specialist, to a lung doctor who ordered surgery. They knew it was cancer, but they didn't know how advanced it was, until they opened him up.

The diagnosis came, they closed him up, the only thing that could be done was for Jimmy to receive rounds of chemotherapy; they would send a specialist. When Jimmy woke up, they were no tubes or needles anywhere, so he knew, there had been any surgery. "What's going on? There are no tubes." He asked me. I had to tell him myself. I held his hand and told him. "Baby," I said, "you have cancer, but we have other options, you can get chemo, there is a doctor that is going to speak to us and explain what can be done."

They ran more tests, and then this very nice lady Doctor Paty, was going to be Jimmy's cancer doctor. She said it was small cell cancer; it was a rapid growing cancer. "If you do nothing, you'll live about three months, you can get chemo and radiation, the cancer could go into remission, or you can live at least one year to fourteen months, if the cancer goes into remission, you can live longer." She said.

Smoking had caught up with Jimmy; he had the kind of cancer that grows fast, small cell cancer, and anyone who says it's my life, well, yes it is, but how many lives are affected in the process of living and dying?

We came, it was February 2005. I told Jimmy "we have to do whatever they say, whatever we are told, so you can live longer." The first thing was to quit smoking, and he tried, I know he tried very hard; he just couldn't beat the habit. Besides that, it was too late now.

We started going to Beaumont for chemo and radiation sessions, we stayed in Beaumont during the week and came home for the weekend. He suffered a lot with the reactions from the chemo; it seems that chemo was worse than the radiation for him. And after six weeks of chemo; He decided to quit the treatment. I fell apart. That meant he wouldn't live but about two months.

We came home, both with our own grieve, I found him in bed; I crawled into bed with him and cried. We both cried our eyes out in each other arms. I told him, "This is not happening to you alone, it's happening to me too." He agreed to get more chemo, Dr. Paty let him rest some and they gave him only radiation for a while.

They took another MRI, it showed the cancer had advanced to his liver. In another six weeks, they ran another MRI, no cancer. We were very happy, somehow I didn't believe it, but Jimmy did.

The house in Kountze was empty; Don was in a Nursing Home. Earl and his wife had decided to get a divorce. So Earl was living at my mother-in law's house. So, when they decided to start Jimmy with chemo again, we went to Kountze, it was a lot closer than Jasper, I called Earl and told him his Daddy didn't want to stay in Beaumont for the chemo, but I thought he would go to Kountze because it was so much closer.

Absolutely, he said, Jimmy agreed to take chemo if we stayed in Kountze with Earl. Beaumont was only 25 minutes from Kountze, he felt better staying there and visiting with Earl every day. We were there on and off about four months, we stayed at Earl's during the week, and come home for the weekends. I would cook dinner and Earl stayed and ate dinner with us. They let him rest for a while.

He kept taking radiation, but no more chemo, they ran another MRI and they found cancerous brain tumor, so they said, they would concentrate in the tumor, the radiation took all his hair, his head was smooth; I remember he was combing his hair over the garbage can so all his hair would fall in it.

September 19. 2005.

Hurricane Rita threatened the Texas and Louisiana coast, our daughter lives in Orangefield, that's on the Texas coast; they had just been evacuated from their home. Hurricane Rita it's going their way, our Son Jimmy works in the Gulf of Mexico, so he had already been evacuated from the rig, and he was on his way home. Lois called. "Mama, can we come home?" she asked, "Of course they could" I went to the store and bought groceries to feed us all for a few days of staying home. This happen before and there has been no problem in Jasper with the storm.

They left home after they secured everything they could. A trip from Orangefield to Jasper its one hour and fifteen minutes, it took them nine hours, because of the traffic. Every once in a while they would call with news they were 50 feet closer. They arrive at our house in the middle of the night, by that time Jasper had been order to evacuate, so we were going to have to leave as well.

When they arrived, they had two other couples and four dogs. I told her, "I can't offer everybody a bed, but I have several couches and reclining chairs. You can sleep there." Jimmy secured his work-shop; his drilling rig was in there. Young Jimmy, Kelvin and the men who came with them brought in a lot of lumber we had outside because we were remodeling a couple of rooms. I also told the women they couldn't bring their dogs in the house. I showed them where the lunch meat was, and told them, to help themselves.

The next day was September 21th, we were all up and about five o'clock in the morning I made coffee for everybody, everyone who wanted a sandwich could make one so we could leave. Young Jimmy bought several 5 gal. Cans of gas, so did Kelvin, we were happy after we saw so many cars off the road out of gas.

Jimmy and I were happy we decided to leave; we were told the hurricane was coming through Jasper, A friend of mine who lives in Waco, Denise Maple, called every hotel in her area, we were in contact with her, the whole time, here was nothing available, the only thing she could find was in Marshall. So she made reservations and we have a place to go to when we arrived. Kelvin and Lois's friends went to Dallas, and Kelvin has a brother in Shreveport, La. They went there. Jimmy was happy our son had decided to stay with us. After they secured the house and the workshop, we left. I stood in front of our house and blessed it; I pray that the Lord guard our Home.

On the way, as soon as we turned into highway 96, we ran into cars on the side of the road all out of gas. The day before we left, Jimmy had gone to the store and came back with several 5 gallons cans filled with gas. We were thankful when we saw how important decision he had made. By the time we arrived to Lufkin, the traffic had slow down, that is the place where people take their highway for other places.

When we arrived to Marshall, the wind was hard that far north and it was raining pretty hard. Television wasn't giving any news about Jasper, but as soon as we knew it had passed, I called the Police Station in Jasper and asked them for news, I told them my husband was on oxygen and he had to have electricity for that. I was told, if you are where you have electricity and water don't come back to Jasper, we have a mess in our hands. He didn't know how long it was going to take to repair all the damage it had to be repaired. We called our own home to hear if the telephone answering machine would answer, we were happy it did.

So, we decided to try to find a small apartment in the area, someone told me to go to a nearby town of Jefferson, we fell in love with the pretty town, it was a lot of history in it. We found a small apartment there; it was two bedrooms, when we open a bank account in Marshall and told the clerk we were moving to Jefferson for a few weeks, she said, "don't rent anything, she said." The Catholic Church has a chapter, St. Vincent de Paul, that help people with furniture, she gave us a phone number and who to call, by this time we were out of our hotel and in a new hotel out the outskirts of Jefferson, the gentleman who we called, came to our motel and asked us what we needed and where to take it. We had never seen so much courtesy and kindness in trying to help someone. And we had never been in a situation like that one. The next day, when we had made all the arrangement to move into our apartment; the gentleman came over with the furniture, beds; a table and chairs for the kitchen, a sofa and a recliner, even linens, and pillows, Jimmy had taken our television set, because it was new. We had also taken our microwave oven. Come to think about it, we took a lot of things in case we didn't have a house to come back to, but with the Lords, help, we didn't even lose a tree. We put a phone in the apartment, my son called his office; they wanted him to go to Lafayette, his port of departure has been Cameron, La. But it disappeared. Cameron was hit first by Katrina and finished it by Rita; there was not a building up in Cameron. So there was a big meeting in Lafayette to find out what they were going to do to get the rigs going because they couldn't get men to the rigs, all ports were badly damaged.

Jimmy and I really enjoyed the time we spent in Jefferson, we visited all the antique shops, I remember they have a General Store, we went in, and every time Jimmy saw something it would remind him at something he had eaten or had as a child or a young man, we had an old time soda, and then we didn't like it, we laughed because we thought it was good then, but not now. We also went to Caddo Lake State Park, we rode for miles, we got lost several times, trying to follow the signs, but I'm sure it was us not been able to follow the signs. We went into their gift shop and bought maps, and T-shirts. As we drove around the park, we ran into many cabins, it was a beautiful and scenic place. Jimmy said, he seemed to remember people talking about, when the first depression happened, they would send men to parks to build cabins such as those, because there were so many people without jobs, and the government, would give them a job, in the parks, and that is how so many parks have cabins next to the water.

Jefferson had a restaurant that everyone who went in started writing their name in the dollar bill and pinned it on the wall. By the time we went in, all the walls were covered. It was difficult to find a place for our dollar bill. Also, there is a train, the caboose of the train, fancy, belong to the owner Jay Gould, and the city of Jefferson bought it because of the history behind it. Jay Gould went to Jefferson in the mid 1800 and offered to let him bring the railroad to Jefferson, but their big Industry was steamboats, and the railroad would kill it. So they turned him down, if you went to Jefferson, Jay Gould wrote in their Hotel registry "the end of Jefferson." It was written after they said no to his offer. Two years later, a huge log jam upstream up Jefferson was dynamited; coming downstream and choking Red River. The River Boats that Jefferson depended on could no longer get to it. While Jefferson shrunk, Shreveport, La. became the new Jefferson. It was never proven that Jay Gould had anything to do with the big log jam explosion, but it fits. And even the other railroad barons didn't want to have anything to do with Gould. The Caboose was closed when we went. I went across to the hotel where the man in charge was. I told him Jimmy didn't always felt like going out, we thought he was open and he was there, could he open the caboose for him? The got his keys out of his pocket and gave them to me. I have pictures of Jimmy opening the caboose with the keys, as we were advancing I kept taking pictures of him in every room. As we were leaving, several women I had seen at the hotel when I was given the keys, they told me the man had said for me to give them the keys, we bring them back to him, they said. I believed the woman, and I gave her the keys. I told Jimmy, "I'm just going to run across the street and thank that man for letting us go into the train. I'll be right back." The woman said, you don't have to do that, I'll thank him for you." I said. "No, I want to thank him myself. "When I did, he said. "I didn't tell her anything." And with that he started to run across the street to get his keys back.

That night, when we went to eat dinner to the restaurant with the dollar bills on the walls, he was there. I apologized to him for giving the keys to the woman. I said. "I'm sorry, but I believed the woman when she told me you had said to get the keys from me." He said. "Lady, they are from New York, they get what they want when they wanted, you're not from New York."

Jimmy had an appointment for a MRI. I called to find out what I could do because we couldn't go to Beaumont. They had a clinic in Longview, we went there, and they sent Jimmy to the VA hospital in Shreveport, La. We went there also, and he had the care that he had missed in Beaumont. There is also a Museum in Jefferson with many old guns, and some Indians relics. Jimmy always loved to visit Museums. In Jefferson, their Industry is Antique Shops, so they have them door to door, at every corner they have a giant hanging basket with beautiful plants of different kind of beautiful flowers. We loved visiting Jefferson. Kelvin and Lois and the children visited us once and we went to have dinner together. Kelvin had come to Jasper because of his mother, Eunice stayed with a friend of hers, what happened with the hurricane Rita never had happened before and not many people believed it would. So many people stayed, then it was hard times, without electricity, the grocery stores could not open, there was no gas because the pumps didn't run without electricity. Then there was no water. He brought them can goods, and everything he could think of because he was told they were starving. There were twelve people in that house, many of them children.

He stopped at our house, without electricity, he had to empty the refrigerator and freezer that I filled before the hurricane; it had to be thrown away. Kelvin also went to their home in Orangefield. They were told there was no way he could access their road, but they went through many detours until finally they were able to get into their street, there were so many trees down everywhere, Lois remembers hearing on Television, Geraldo Rivera could not get into their area because there were so many trees down. When we spoke with Kelvin again he said, even your bird feeder its standing.

Jimmy made it back to Jefferson; he said the roads were all impassable, it was very hard to go through just about anywhere you wanted to go without having to detour somewhere; Until he made it there. Jimmy liked Jefferson so much, he considered moving there, what stopped him were the trains, they blow their whistle all the time, day and night, and stop you on the road everywhere.

We called our friends all the time, trying to find out how they were, the ones that had stayed in Jasper. They all had a story about how hard it was to be in Jasper under those circumstances. I tried to find out when it was safe for us to come home, we were very thankful we had left, I am certain Jimmy would had never survived that kind of punishment. Then, the electrical company said, our home had electricity, four weeks after the hurricane.

The trip back was not bad at the beginning, but as we approached Jasper, we could see the was devastation signs of the trees over houses, so many crushed roofs, some roads still had signs of trees on them. As we got closer to Jasper, some road couldn't be crossed, it was a sad sight, trees were everywhere; it will be many years before the timber industry recovers. A friend of mine told me the day after the hurricane, people got out of their houses, and they couldn't get out of their yard with trees everywhere blocking the streets. They went back in and came back out with their saws to saw the trees and open the way to the neighbors and look at each other.

We made it home, we were very happy and thankful everything was in place at home. We were so glad Jimmy had decided to stay with us; there were so many things we couldn't have done had it not being for him. It was good to sleep in our bed again.

It was November, Rosi came over to visit with us, and she was here over the Thanksgiving holidays, really, she was here to say good bye to Jimmy, of course nothing liked that was mentioned. We went to the Mall in Beaumont, I never thought Jimmy would stay thirty minutes, but we stayed several hours. Lois got him a wheelchair so he could go where ever we wanted to go. He laughed at people's funny way to dress, or whatever he thought it was funny. We always enjoyed cappuccino coffee and had some there at the bookstore's coffee shop. We both enjoyed Rosi's visit, Lois and her family and Jimmy were all here for Thanksgiving.

I called Lois and told her, "Daddy wants to quit the treatment again." She said "Mama, it's his life; you have to let him go. "But I couldn't, I just couldn't do that.

December was here, Kelvin carved a beautiful figure of a bride and groom kissing for our wedding anniversary, Lois and her family were here, Jimmy was working. "We celebrated Christmas, all the kids were here. We had a good Christmas.

Everybody came for our New Year's celebration; Earl and his girlfriend Dana were here as well. Everybody took a lot of pictures, and he let us.

Jimmy had one more appointment, he thought he would fulfill, they took an MRI, when the results came back, they say saw progress cancer wasn't growing; they couldn't make him take the treatment. And so, Jimmy decided to continue with the treatment it was only radiation. This time we would, instead of staying in Kountze, we stayed with Alexys and her family. It was closer and so we stayed in Orangefield for several weeks. When we stayed at Lois's house Lauren was fifteen years old, Kyle was twelve years old. In January 2006, he started with radiation for a brain tumor.

**Alexys, with her family, her husband Kelvin,
and their children Lauren and Kyle.**

Jimmy works for a different company now; he is safety man and living in Jasper.

It was the third or fourth week since we were staying at Lois's house, and it was Valentine's Day, when we got back from Jimmy's radiation session, I went to our bedroom to put up my purse, when I got to the dining room where Jimmy had gone to, with the rest of the family, Jimmy's right arm was shaking quite badly, then his right leg started to shake violently, his whole right side, we called the clinic but it had slowed down enough that he said it was okay.

But started again, it was after 5:00 p.m. Kelvin, suggested to call an Ambulance, Lois and I were so out of it, that all we thought about was to take him to Emergency, at that time of the day, it would had been impossible in the evening traffic. The Ambulance came, by that time, Jimmy was hollering, "Make it stop, I want this to stop." I have never felt so useless, for not been able to do something in my life, not being able to help Jimmy was killing me. When the Ambulance arrived, they couldn't do anything either. A doctor had to see

Jimmy, somehow they got him in the Ambulance, the medics from the Ambulance said it was a seizure, by that time Jimmy was shaking uncontrollably; I rode in the front of the Ambulance.

He was taken to a hospital in Port Arthur, probably because it was closer, with the traffic, it would have taken longer. They went to work on him as soon as we arrived. It was very difficult to get a vein. But somehow they did. Very slowly Jimmy stop shaking and went to sleep.

Later that night, when he was stabilized, they moved him to Beaumont, St. Elizabeth Hospital. Our Priest came over to visit Jimmy, I have not emphasized our faith, but our Priest baptized Jimmy a few years back, July 1995, and when Jimmy couldn't go to church, Father Ron Foshage would come to the house and bring Jimmy communion, like in this case, all the way to Beaumont.

Jimmy's medication for seizure had its side effect, hallucinations. Funny thing was that he had a name for everybody, even Lois, but he always knew who I was. He said, "Baby, no one can get up to your heels, you're always above everyone else." I didn't notice what he was doing, categorizing everybody, anytime someone would come in, he would come up with a story in reference of them. Lois told me. We stayed in the hospital one week, we came home, and nurses would come to check him out because there are things I don't know how to do. But he told me. "Baby, I don't want to go back to the hospital." I knew he didn't want more needles. So, I said. "Whatever you want James, it will be done."

It was March 8th my birthday, he bought me two dozen roses; they took several pictures of us with the roses. Then, his buddies from work came over to visit with him. They spent the whole day with him. I told him it was my birthday present to him. Jimmy and his friends made an agreement. Jimmy's beloved rig would go to the Houston office and be displayed there; a plaque will be place on it. He was satisfied his life labor would not stay and catch dust after he was gone. It was his legacy.

After a couple of weeks of nurses that came only every once in a while, I was ready for hospice to come in. Doctors' had advised that earlier, but I knew it meant it was the end for Jimmy and I didn't want it to be. I wasn't ready for that, but I knew I would never be ready for it.

Lois moved in, she knew before I did the end was near, I guess I couldn't admit it to myself, she said she wanted to be near her Daddy, after about a week. Jimmy asked us to call Jimmy off the rig. He came the next day. Jimmy felt better by Monday. He went back to work. Lois felt a bad cold coming down and she left with ten minutes, she was out of here.

That night neither one of us could sleep; we came to the kitchen to talk. He looked around the kitchen. I asked him if he wanted anything. He said. "I want a drink." I said. "I don't know how to fix you a drink, but I bring the stuff and you tell me what to put in." I brought a toll glass, a bottle of whiskey, and ice, he gave me the amounts he wanted, and he wanted water in it, and he asked for a cigarette. Then I placed my chair very close to his, and he talked like he had never done before.

I only said, "How am I going to live without you?"

He said, "You are strong, Baby, you can make it, and Baby, go home, go home and be with your family. I know you have been away much too long." And it was true. I have not been to Mexico in eight years because I wouldn't go without him. He knew it. His body couldn't handle the altitude of Mexico City. Lois, Jimmy and Kelvin, tried to get me to go years ago, they said they wouldn't leave Jimmy alone so I would go. I said, "No, I need to be here, please, don't ask me again."

The following Friday, he said again, call Jimmy again, Lois made the call. This time, Lois called Earl and Robert as well. By the way, Lois was so sick when she left, by the next day, she was fine and was able to come back, and we believe it was Jimmy needed to talk to me, had Lois being home. He wouldn't have done it.

My family called constantly to check on Jimmy. I stayed with Jimmy in bed, I never left him. When I thought he was sleep, I got up and went to the bathroom, I was brushing my teeth when the nurse told me, he is looking for you. I said. "I'm coming Baby, I'm just brushing my teeth." The nurse told me, If I hadn't seen it with my own eyes, I wouldn't have believe that he was able to sit up in bed by himself when he felt I wasn't in bed with him. Earlier, he was facing me, in bed, and the nurse thought I had placed him like that, when I told her he did it by himself she told my daughter I was hallucinating and that I had turned him myself.

I read the Bible to him and told him Corky would be waiting for him and his mama, and his father and brothers that had gone ahead of him. He nodded. His last words were. "I love you." Our son Jimmy arrived Saturday, so he was here Sunday, his brother Robert and his wife Iris came, then Earl came, he went to talk to him in the bedroom, I told him, he can't answer you, but he can hear you, they stayed for a while and then left.. at 6:35 p.m. on Sunday April 2nd 2006, my beloved Jimmy died. Both our children and grandchildren were here, and Kelvin. I heard myself screamed; I didn't know I was screaming.

Many years ago, when Jimmy had a heart attack, I told Sandy Stark, a good friend of mine, I always said Jimmy has a heart of gold, but is melting........and now, it has.

Epilogue

After the funeral and everyone had left, it was the big test of being alone, really alone.

I couldn't sleep; I would stay awake until two or three in the morning. One of the nurses decided to move Jimmy to my side of the bed so he wouldn't get bruise; within thirty minutes, he died, he was on my side of the bed when he died, that's why I couldn't lie down on my side of the bed, or on his either. Finally, I decided to go home, two and a half months after Jimmy's death. I would stay one week with my sister, two days with a cousin, a week with a niece, I also visited Amalia, Esperanza and Lucila, when I went to Coatzacoalcos, I stayed at Rosi's house, I met with school friends, one of my classmates recognized me and made a few calls, when we met at a restaurant, we were eight, from third and fourth grade. We met four times in the month I was In Coatzacoalcos. I found out they are still meeting, I'm so glad I started that.

My father was from the State of Michoacan, and we never went because all his sisters lived in Mexico City, so I wanted to go there, Raul and Esperanza's daughter Lucila, invited us to go, it was seven of us on the trip. They have a beautiful SUV so it was plenty of room for all of us, Raul Jr. drove us there. It really was the highlight of my trip to Mexico, my family never left me alone, while I was in Coatzacoalcos, I went to Veracruz with Ramon and Rosi, among other places they took me. My niece, Reyna Patricia lives in Leon

Guanajuato, it was a nice trip, Amalia lives in Queretaro, close to the Pacific coast of Mexico. I stayed three months. But when I came back, I was a lone again.

Since I couldn't sleep, somehow, I thought of putting a cookbook together for my church to help the needed, I gathered 300 recipes, some from the church, some of my friends from overseas, Beryl and her daughter Carolynne sent me recipes. Beryl has entered recipes in cooking contests, and won many times, she sent me those recipes. There are recipes from Mexico, Spain, Australia, so the book has sold very well. Now staying up until two or three o'clock in the morning, had a meaning.

I have a few things "happening" to me since Jimmy passed away, I continually talk to Jimmy, I asked him "if you are with me give me a sign." Once, the phone rang, when I answered it had hung up, I look for the name of the caller, it was James Moore, so I thought I missed my son's call from the rig. I picked up the receiver to look at the number; it said James R. Moore and our home phone number. How can that be? I called the phone company and asked the operator, "Are there any lines being repaired in this are?" I asked the operator. She checked in our area, she said. "No, there are no repairs being done in your area. I have no answer for you Mrs. Moore." Several people had said to me, you have your sign, Blanca." I had my own telephone number in my receiver for a while and would look at it often, I couldn't believe it.

A friend of mine I met while Jimmy and I stayed in Beaumont during his chemo sessions, invited me to go on a cruise, to Yucatan in March, I said, if it was another time, but it's just before Jimmy's anniversary of his death. I can't go, I told her. She said its only one week, we'll be back before April 1st. my children encouraged me to go. So, I said, okay. And I started to make the arrangements for the trip, my friend ordered the tickets, and I was getting excited about being on the cruise.

Then I went to lunch with a group of friends, we started talking about the women in the Bible, about the woman who married seven brothers, and she asked the Lord with whom would she reunite in heaven? And the Lord response was. With none of them. I said to her, "When I die, I'm going to reunite with Jimmy."

She said, "No, you'll never see Jimmy again." I became very upset, I don't care what you say, I didn't marry seven brothers, I only married Jimmy. I told her. I will reunite with Jimmy. When I left to get my car, a friend of mine walked with me, she told me, don't pay any attention to her.

But I couldn't help myself, I couldn't stop crying, I decided I wasn't going on the cruise. I was as bad as I was in the beginning. I cried myself to sleep. And when I did, Jimmy was in bed with me, this was the first time I dreamt with him, he had a light like illuminated him, and he had his beautiful smile, he was looking at me and when I saw him, he got closer to me and embraced me, like he always did. We always slept in each other arms.

When I woke up in the morning, I was fresh again. The heavy load in my heart had left me, and I was ready to go on the cruise, and I did.